The Thomas Coram Research Unit, at the Institute of Education, University of London, was founded in 1971 by Professor Jack Tizard. It is a centre of conceptual and methodological expertise in the study of families, the development of children and the care of children outside their families. It has a strong orientation to policy-relevant research in the areas of welfare, health and education services, out-of-school care and recreation services for school-age children, the changing economic and social circumstances of families, drug prevention programmes, adolescent health and parenting, parental control within the family, early intervention with reading difficulties, classroom experience of infant school pupils and public law aspects of the Children Act.

The Unit is multi-disciplinary and applies a wide range of methods, from case studies to secondary analysis of large-scale data sets. It has extensive international interests, and two important European networks – on school-age childcare and on the reconciliation of employment and family life – are coordinated from the Unit. A Centre for Research in Family Life and Employment has also recently been established in the Unit.

### Books published by HMSO for the TCRU

1. Playgroups in a Changing World   0 11 321303 4   *1990*
2. Playgroups in Practice   0 11 321498 7   *1992*
3. Current Issues in Day Care for Young Children   0 11 321337 9   *1991*
4. Play and Care   0 11 701844 9   *1994*
5. Implementing the Children Act for Children under 8   0 11 701971 2   *1994*
6. Staff: Child Ratios in Care and Education Services for Young Children   0 11 701972 0   *1994*

   All HMSO books are available through Accredited Agents and good booksellers

### Other relevant publications from members of TCRU

7. Edward Melhuish and Peter Moss (eds) (*1991*) Day Care for Young Children: International Perspectives, London: Routledge
8. Eilis Hennessy, Sue Martin, Peter Moss and Edward Melhuish (*1992*) Children and Day Care: Lessons from Research, London: Paul Chapman

9. Peter Moss and Alan Pence (eds) (1994) Valuing Quality in Early Childhood Services, London: Paul Chapman

# Implementing the Children Act for Children Under 8

**Research carried out by the Thomas Coram Research Unit on behalf of the Department of Health**

**Julie Bull**

**Claire Cameron**

**Mano Candappa**

**Peter Moss**

**Charlie Owen**

**June Statham**

London: HMSO

ISBN 0 11 701971 2

# Contents

# Acknowledgments

The authors would like to thank the Department of Health for funding the project. Thanks in particular go to Carolyn Davies at the Department of Health, for guidance and support, and to all members of the project advisory group. We are also grateful to colleagues Peter Elfer, Gillian Pugh and Susan McQuail at the Early Childhood Unit at the National Children's Bureau for their helpful advice and comments. Helen Penn, as consultant to the project, has also provided invaluable support and expertise. Sofia Ali has provided administrative support to the project since it began and has helped in the production of this report of the first stage.

Finally, our gratitude goes to all the local authorities who have participated in the first stage of the study and to individual respondents from these authorities who gave up their valuable time to share their experiences of implementing the Act with us. The information and insights they have provided form the basis of this report.

# List of abbreviations

| | |
|---|---|
| DfE | Department for Education |
| DES | Department of Education and Science |
| DHSS | Department of Health and Social Security |
| DoH | Department of Health |
| DSS | Department of Social Security |
| FTE | Full-time Equivalent |
| GHS | General Household Survey |
| IPPR | Institute of Public Policy Research |
| MYM | MUDIAD YSGOLION MEITHRIN |
| NCMA | National Childminding Association |
| NHS | National Health Service |
| OPCS | Office of Population Censuses and Surveys |
| PPA | Preschool Playgroups Association |
| SSI | Social Services Inspectorate |
| TCRU | Thomas Coram Research Unit |
| TEC | Training and Enterprise Council |
| The Guidance | *Guidance and Regulations to the Children Act (Vol. 2): Family Support, Day Care and Educational Provision for Young Children* |
| UNICEF | United Nations Children's Fund |

# Summary of Main Findings

This report presents interim results from a study being undertaken by the Thomas Coram Research Unit (TCRU) on the implementation of the Children Act as it affects day care and educational provision for young children. The study is being undertaken in a sample of English local authorities, and the report includes material from a linked study being carried out in all local authorities in Wales. The results published in this report are from the first stage of the studies, which focused on how local authorities have implemented the Act. The second stage, currently under-way, will assess the impact of the Act on services provided for young children. The first stage is based very largely on interviews with local authority officers engaged in implementation. The perspectives of organis-ations and individuals from outside the local authority will be explored in the second stage of the studies.

In general, the first stage of the study, conducted around a year after implementation of the Act had begun, shows that the Act was widely welcomed by local authority staff involved in under-8s services. The general perception was that the Act had put services for young children 'on the map' and had gone some way to ending their historically marginal role. The enthusiasm with which the Act was greeted has resulted in the investment of a great deal of time and energy in efforts to turn the promise of the legislation into effective policies and practice. This is despite a general climate of change and financial constraint in most local authorities.

*Coordination*

- Coordinating structures remained patchy. Most had been in place before the Act and were primarily intended to provide opportunities for the exchange and dissemination of information rather than being a means for developing a coordinated approach to the development of policy and the deployment of resources

- In general, implementing the Act had been perceived as coming under the jurisdiction of the Social Services Department, and there were few examples of the 'corporate approach' to implementation urged in *Guidance and Regulations to the Children Act* (hereafter referred to as 'the Guidance'). In this respect, Wales differed somewhat to England, with more emphasis placed on a multi-agency approach to implementation.

- The implementation of the Act, and in particular the subsequent publication by all authorities of the review, had stimulated inter-departmental communication. While coordination was the most frequent theme of recommendations in reviews, at this early stage there was little evidence that improved communication had led to more coordinated action: for example, there were few examples of initiatives such as joint policy statements or joint admissions criteria.

- A number of factors impeded coordination, including different philosophies of different government departments, the impact of other legislation and reforms, and inadequate resources.

- The value of the review exercise was widely acknowledged, but reviews themselves had often been carried out quickly and with very limited resources, were mainly descriptive rather than analytical and few had specific recommendations – on costings and timings, for example.

*Provision*

- Definitions of need had, in general, been drawn up within Social Services Departments with some exceptions. Wales had more commonly adopted an inter-agency approach to the task than had English authorities, and this was thought to have been useful in facilitating the debate about children's services.

- In following through their duty to provide services for children in need, local authorities had adopted a range of different approaches to defining need. These ranged from 'restrictive' interpretations which simply prioritised children who were at risk or who were Social Services clients, to adopting broad continuums of need which incorporated socio-economic factors such as poverty. These differences reflected a general tension between the desire to adopt broad, non-stigmatising definitions and the need to ration scarce resources.

- Despite having reformulated definitions of need and priorities for access to services, local authorities had not, for the most part, translated these policies into practice through altering their assessment processes at this stage.

- Local authorities had experienced difficulties with identifying overall levels of need, and some had made little or no progress with this.

- Little progress had been made by authorities on the compilation of registers of children with disabilities, nor were there any substantial changes to policy of provision in respect of day care for children with disabilities other than some additional sponsored places with child-minders and playgroups.

- Although precise financial data is difficult to obtain, it was generally reported that lack of resources for provision of day care were making it difficult to develop or expand day care for children in need or other children. Reductions in overall departmental budgets were more likely to result in pressure to reduce support for voluntary sector provision of various kinds.

*Regulation and support*

- The new regulatory provisions contained in the Act had resulted in a significant reorganisation of registration and inspection in most local authorities. This had involved mobilising extra resources of various kinds in most cases, and was generally thought to have resulted in improvements to the efficiency and effectiveness of the regulatory system.

- There were great variations in the way in which regulation had been organised and staffed which are likely to have significant implications for practice. The most notable of these organisational differences was the organisation of inspection which was either organised at 'arm's length' from the service provider or kept in locally based teams.

- The level of consultation with and participation of other agencies and providers in developing local standards was varied. Those authorities who had consulted widely believed this to have been the key to successful implementation of the standards.

- There was no evidence of local authorities applying standards above those set out in the Guidance. Nor was there any significant evidence of closure of provision through cancellation/refusal of registration at this stage. Most authorities believed themselves to be flexible and encouraging in their approach and were consequently surprised by Circular 1/93 which suggested they had been otherwise.

- With a few exceptions, there was little evidence of increased support for providers becoming available as a result of the Act. In fact, in many authorities, the extra emphasis on regulation was thought to have reduced the staff time available for support and, in some independent inspection units, support provision was generally thought to be in conflict with the regulation role. The availability of support, training and advice for providers therefore remained very varied between areas, or even between districts, despite the need for such support being more acute in the light of new regulatory provisions.

*Ethnic diversity*

- The emphasis within the Act and accompanying Guidance on the need to pay attention to racial, cultural and linguistic diversity has forced many local authorities to address equal opportunities issues in relation to under-eights services for the first time. Policy developments in this area, however, were uneven, and there were few examples of how policy might effect change in practice or in service delivery at this stage. Consultation with minority ethnic communities had clearly proved difficult.

*Rural areas*

- Finally, the Act potentially offered the opportunity to address some of the issues facing children in rural areas through its emphasis on coordination over implementation with and support of providers. The review, in particular, enabled local authorities to highlight gaps in provision for such children. Working against this, however, was the need to target resources to children in need, definitions of whom often excluded or overlooked the needs of children living in isolated rural areas.

Chapter

# 1    Introduction

The Children Act 1989 was implemented in October 1991. The Children Bill, which predated it, was described by the Lord Chancellor as the 'most comprehensive and far-reaching reform of child care law which has come before Parliament in living memory'. Its scope was indeed comprehensive. It sought to unite a fragmented body of public and private law under a single statute, in which 'the law provides a single, rationalised child care system, with all legal remedies available in all cases' (Fox-Harding, 1991). Within its broad remit, the Act included sections that dealt specifically with day care services for children under 8 years – in particular sections within Part III ('Local Authority Support for Children and Families') and Part X ('Childminding and Day Care for Young Children').

Two studies are being undertaken by the Thomas Coram Research Unit (TCRU) to examine the implementation of the Act **as it affects day care and educational provision for young children**. One study is being undertaken in Wales, funded by the Welsh Office; the second study focuses on England and is funded by the Department of Health (DoH). The results of the study in Wales have been reported more fully elsewhere (Statham, 1993), and this report focuses primarily on the findings from the first stage of the English study. The first stage has concentrated on **how local authorities have implemented the Act**. The second stage, currently underway, will assess **the impact of the Act** on day care and education services for young children.

**The research project**

The main sources of information for the first stage of the study were interviews with officers, and sometimes other respondents, in 26 local authorities across England and Wales, which included 18 English authorities and all eight Welsh counties. Relevant documents were also collected from these local authorities. The findings are set in the context of analysis of statistics on levels of preschool provision taken from the TCRU's computerised database on day care and education services for young children in each authority in England and Wales.

The 18 English authorities represented a stratified random sample of one in six local authorities. To obtain this sample local authorities were stratified into five groups – inner and outer London boroughs, metropolitan districts, and northern and southern counties. A similar proportion of authorities were chosen from each group, ensuring coverage of a cross-section representing many localities, from inner cities to small towns and sparsely populated rural districts. This enabled the study's results to be applied to the country as a whole with a high degree of confidence.

Each local authority was visited by a member of the research team, usually over a period of two or three days. The visit was arranged through the Director of Social Services. Follow-up phone calls sought 'key people' who would best be able to answer questions about the implementation of the Children Act in the study's area of interest. The number of key people interviewed in each local authority ranged from four to nine and included at least one officer in the Education Department. Officers from other departments or elected members were included where they had played a prominent role in implementation. Although a limited number of voluntary sector representatives were interviewed during the first stage where they had been heavily involved in local authority implementation, on the whole the perspectives of those outside the local authority remain to be explored in the second stage of the study.

A fuller picture of the exact numbers of respondents interviewed and their location within the authorities is provided in Appendix A. The broad topics covered with respondents are outlined in Appendix B. The data for analysis were taken from tape-recordings and notes made during interview. Relevant policy documents were collected by researchers in advance of the visits where possible, and many more documents were gathered during and after the visit and were included in the final analysis.

Fieldwork in the authorities took place over a six-month period between September 1992 and March 1993, the period during which local authorities faced statutory deadlines for the completion of the first review and the re-registration of existing day care provision. It is important to bear in mind that the findings reported here present the picture at a particular stage – around one year after the implementation of the Act. Moreover, because local authorities were seen over a six-month period, the stages of response to the Act varied. Finally, in considering the timing of this fieldwork period, the Children Act was not the only item on the agendas of local authorities. It was a time of considerable change within local authorities, involving major restructuring of many Social Services and Education Departments, conflicting demands from other pieces of important legislation and impending local government reorganisation.

**The Act: duties and powers**

The Children Act, in conjunction with the Education Act 1980 (which confers on local education authorities the power to decide whether or not to provide nursery education for children under 5), gives local authorities three main functions in respect of services for children under 8: **to coordinate provision** made by different agencies; **to provide services** for children in need; and **to regulate provision** offered by the private and voluntary sectors. More specifically, the Children Act gives local authorities a number of duties and powers in respect of day care services and educational provision for young children.

Duties include:

- a general duty to provide day care (and other) services for children who are in need and their families (Sections 17,18), to publicise the services available to families with children in need, and to have regard for the different racial groups in the area to which children in need belong (Schedule 2)

- a duty to regulate most private and voluntary day care services (Part X)

- a duty (jointly by Social Services and Education Departments) to conduct a review of day care provision used by under-8s in the area at least once every three years (Section 19).

Powers include:

- the power to provide day care for children not in need (Section 18)

- the power to provide support services (facilities such as training, guidance and counselling) for adults working in a day care setting (Section 18).

The Act needs to be considered together with two subsequent and complementary documents. The **Children Act Guidance and Regulations (Vol. 2)** (hereafter referred to as the 'Guidance') is *'intended to provide a clear statement of the requirements placed on local authorities by the Children Act . . . and discuss the implications for policy and practice'*. **Circular 1/93** was issued to local authorities in January 1993. It was intended to *'clarify the general purpose and application of the Guidance . . . give further Guidance on the day care review duty . . . and contains additional and amended Guidance on certain matters relating to registration standards and requirements'*. In particular, it urged local authorities to adopt 'flexibility' in the application of standards and reminded local authorities that standards in Guidance were not legally required.

**The context for the Children Act**

Understanding the context in which the Children Act has been implemented helps to assess the significance of the Act, to identify the opportunities it offers as well as its limitations, and to appreciate what external factors might constrain or enhance the impact of the Act.

## Day care policies

There are three major features of policy on day care services[1], and all three go back many years. First, there is public responsibility for the provision of day care services, which is limited to the welfare function (children and families 'in need'); otherwise, provision is considered to be a private matter for which parents have financial responsibility (c.f. Education Select Committee 1989, p. 197; Ministry of Health Circular 37/68). Second, there is a public duty to regulate most day care services (Ibid.). Finally, coordination between statutory and independent agencies concerned with day care and other services for young children is encouraged, although on the basis that 'day care' and 'education' for children under 5 are legally, administratively and conceptually distinct (c.f. Education Select Committee, 1989, p. 199; Hansard, 4.2.91, p. 68).

In this context, it can be seen that the Act mainly consolidates, rather than reforms, the basic structure of existing policy on day care. Indeed, retaining the concept of 'day care' in the Act and placing 'day care' services into an essentially welfare measure like the Children Act reaffirms a perspective that 'day care' is a distinct and valid concept and that 'care' and 'education' for young children are separable. By contrast, two other countries which made major reforms of services for young children at the same time as the Children Act was implemented based their reforms on a perspective that 'care' and 'education' were inseparable, placed responsibility for all services for children under compulsory school age with one department (Education) and developed a new concept to encompass all services for children up to 5 years: 'early childhood care and education' in New Zealand; 'educacio infantil' in Spain.

The Children Act is, however, innovatory in certain important details: for example, its strengthening of regulation; the aspirations (in the Guidance) to use regulation to promote quality; its recognition of ethnic diversity, both in relation to children 'in need' and regulation; its concern to make services more responsive to the needs of ethnic minority families; and the introduction of the Section 19 review.

## Day care services

Day care and education services for young children, and their development during the 1980s, are discussed in detail in the next chapter. Here, it is relevant to note three features of the services provided prior to the Act (for

1.  The main types of provision to be included under the heading of 'day care services' are day nurseries, playgroups, child-minders and out-of-school clubs and holiday schemes.

fuller discussion and references, see Chapter 2). First, day care services, with which the Act primarily deals, play a major role in providing for children under 5, partly because of the limited development of nursery schooling; in particular, playgroups provide for more children than any other type of service. Second, day care services are very largely provided within an unsubsidised private market, so that they depend on parental ability to pay. The fastest growth in service since the 1980s has occurred in this sector, due to the rapid growth of child-minders and, in particular, private day nurseries. While private day care services have many strengths and virtues, many of them are poorly resourced with respect to training, pay and conditions, accommodation and other material circumstances. These features of the service context have particular implications for regulation and support. Finally, there has been an uneven development of services, both public and private, between local authorities. In implementing the Act, therefore, local authorities start from very different points.

*Legislative and administrative context*

The Children Act has been implemented in the context of extensive legislative and administrative changes which affect local authorities in many ways and have specific implications for the implementation of the Act. During the period immediately preceding the Children Act, and during its implementation, local authorities have had to take on board a range of other major pieces of legislation. Within Social Services, there has been the National Health Service and Community Care Act 1991 and the Criminal Justice Act 1991; Education Departments have faced seven major legislative reforms since the early 1980s. Boundary changes to local authorities have also been proposed, with implications for planning and coordination. All of these have impinged on local authorities' resources, and at times have involved conflicting demands. For example, while the Children Act specified 'working together' across departments, the Education Reform Act encouraged schools to disengage from local education authorities, thus reducing their strategic influence and making it unclear how authorities could work together in practice.

Day care services and educational provision for young children have traditionally involved two government departments (in England) – the Department of Health and the Department for Education. However, recently, and coinciding with the implementation of the Children Act, other public bodies have developed an interest in day care services. At central government level, these include: the Employment Department, with its Out-of-School Childcare Initiative (announced in 1992 and started in 1993); the Department of Social Security, which will provide a limited subsidy for child care costs for one group of benefit claimants, by taking account of these costs (up to a certain level) for Family Credit recipients (announced in the November 1993 budget, to be introduced in 1994); and, most recently, the Prime Minister's office, with its interest in nursery education (*Sunday Times*, 26.12.93). At a local level, Training and Enterprise Councils (TECs) and local authority units concerned with employment and economic development have become involved with the Out-of-School Initiative, but also with day care services for younger children. Overall, therefore the Children Act has been implemented in a context of proliferating interest groups. What makes this proliferation particularly significant is the absence of any overarching concept, policy or responsibility to encompass the full range of services for young children.

### Family trends

The 1980s and 1990s have seen a number of significant trends in family life. Each contributes an important part to the context within which the Children Act was conceived and implemented, producing new circumstances, needs and demands, and these trends are relevant in particular to the provision and regulation of services for young children.

The first of these trends has been a rapid increase, since 1985, in employment among women with young children. Between 1973 and 1985, the employment rate for mothers with children under 5 increased only from 25% to 30%; but between 1985 and 1991, it increased from 30% to 43%. Moreover, while most employed mothers had part-time jobs in 1991, full-time employment grew at twice the rate of part-time employment between 1985 and 1991 (Bridgwood and Savage, 1993, Table 5.11). However, this growth in employment was not uniform. Employment grew fastest among women with high qualifications, living in two-parent families, with a partner in employment; it grew least, or even declined, among lone mothers, Afro-Caribbean mothers, and women with no qualifications and those with non-employed partners (Harrop and Moss, 1994).

The second trend, which is by now well known, is the substantial increase in lone-parent families. Between 1971 and 1981, the proportion of such families grew from 8% to 13%, a rise of 63%. Over the next ten years, the increase was from 13% to 19%, a rise of 46%. However, nearly all of the increase during the 1980s has occurred since 1987; between then and 1991, lone parenthood has increased from 14% to 19% (Bridgwood and Savage, 1993; Table 2.18).

Finally, the 1980s witnessed a large increase in poverty among families with children (O'Higgins and Jenkins, 1989; Bradshaw, 1990; Cornia, 1990;

IPPR, 1993; Kumar, 1993). A recent report from the National Children's Bureau concludes that *'the number of children living in poverty increased threefold in the period 1979–90/91, from 10% to over 30% of the population, with another 10% living on the margin of poverty'* (Kumar 1993, p. 187). The report further concludes that *'children of minority ethnic groups stood a significantly higher risk of living in poverty'* (Ibid., p. 188).

This trend of rising poverty among children and their families has been due to a number of factors including relatively high levels of unemployment; an increase in the incidence of low pay; and an increase in the number of lone-parent families. The growth in poverty has not been unique to Britain; poverty has increased since the mid-1970s in many countries. However, a recent United Nations Children's Fund (UNICEF) report concludes that the increase has been most pronounced in Ireland and the United Kingdom (Cornia, 1990).

**The structure of the report**

The next chapter analyses the trends in day care and education provision for young children over the last decade. The rest of the report is mainly given over to presenting findings from the first stage of the studies in England and Wales and shows how local authorities have gone about implementation of the Act in respect of their three main functions: coordination (Chapter 3), provision (Chapter 4) and regulation (Chapter 5). Other chapters report on two specific themes which have been identified by the two studies as particularly important: equal opportunities and ethnic diversity (Chapter 6) and rural areas (Chapter 7).

# Trends in Early Childhood Services 1982–92

**Introduction**

In March 1992 in England, there were places for about 40% of the total child population aged 0–4 in 'early childhood services' – 780,900 places in 'day care' services (i.e. playgroups, day nurseries and child-minders) and 515,955 in schools (i.e. in nursery education or reception classes) (see Table 2.1a). A further 59,400 places were available in out-of-school clubs and holiday schemes for children aged 5–7.

In Wales, the overall level of provision is higher, with places in 'early childhood services' for 43% of the total under 5 population. There are higher levels of school provision in Wales. The 43,494 places in schools are equivalent to 23% of the 0–4 population in Wales, while school places in England are equivalent to only 16% of the population. In contrast, the 39,372 places in 'day care' services in Wales are proportionately fewer than in England (equivalent to 20% of the 0–4 population, compared to 24% in England). There is no information on out-of-school clubs and holiday schemes in Wales.

However, this apparently clear-cut statement of affairs, based on annual statistics collected and published by the Department of Health (1993b), the Department for Education (1993) and the Welsh Office (1993a, b), disguises a more complicated situation.

**Statistical sources and their limitations**

Tables 2.1 and 2.2 show places in a wide variety of services for England and Wales: day nurseries (local authority and independent, registered) playgroups, child-minders, maintained nursery education and reception classes, and private schools. However, a number of qualifications should be made. Firstly, the tables do not cover all services providing day care for young children: home-based care by 'nannies' is missing; so too is the number of places in local authority family centres and in independent services that do not have to be registered.

Second, the statistics in England come from two sources (the Department of Health (DoH) and Department for Education (DfE)) and are not comparable in important respects. Although statistics for day care and schools in Wales come from a single source (the Welsh Office), they are presented in different formats which are also not comparable. DfE and Welsh Office statistics for maintained and private schools present the number of pupils, not the number of places. This is significant since many pupils attend on a part-time basis: nearly 300,000 in England (89% of the total in maintained nursery education, 36% in private schools and 9% in reception classes) and just over 40,000 in Wales (73%, 18% and 2% respectively). Calculating places (the actual volume of service) from statistics on pupils using those places involves making the assumption that two part-time pupils occupy each place – a reasonable assumption for nursery education but less certain for private schools and reception classes.

The Department of Health, on the other hand, generally presents statistics in the form of places. The main exception is local authority day nurseries, where the number of children attending is also published. Comparing statistics in England for local authority day nursery places (23,800) and children attending (28,400) shows that each nursery place is used, on average, by 1.2 children; in Wales, which had far lower levels of provision, the average was 1.7. The same may apply for other types of day care services, but no information is given in the official DoH statistics. However, the regular statistical review by the Preschool Playgroups Association (PPA) of its members reveals that each place in a playgroup is used, on average, by 1.8 children (PPA, 1993). In both nursery classes and playgroups therefore, the majority of places are part-time.

Third, we have presented child-minders as if they provided exclusively for children under 5, but of the 252,100 places registered in England in 1992, nearly a third (77,000) were classified as being 'for children 0–7'; the remaining places were classified as 'for children under 5 only'. There is however no way of knowing, from the DoH statistics, what proportion of the 77,700 places are actually used by children under 5 or between 5 and 7, and indeed the proportion may fluctuate over time. Welsh Office statistics for 1992 give places only for children aged 0–7.

Finally, the statistics for child-minders presented in Tables 2.1a and 2.1b also represent the situation as recorded by local authorities in 1992, before the re-registration of child-minders was complete. As Chapter 5 notes in more detail, this exercise revealed that many of these child-minders were not actually active. The figures for 1993 may therefore give a more accurate picture of the number of places provided by child-minders.

**The supply of services**

Tables 2.2a and 2.2b show the growth in supply of services for children under 5 between 1982 and 1992, the decade before implementation of the

Children Act, for England and Wales. They also show that in this period there was substantial growth in the number of children under 5. The supply of services has had to increase by 14% in England and 12% in Wales between 1982 and 1992 simply to keep up with this growth.

In this period, there was low growth or actual decline in two services: playgroups and local authority day nurseries. The low growth in play-group places in the 1980s can perhaps be seen as a combination of the effects of steady growth in school provision, which is in direct competition with playgroups for the 3–4 year age group, and of saturated provision following years of very rapid growth in the 1960s and 1970s. Within playgroups there has been a growth in 'extended daycare' and 'full day care' playgroups. The number of PPA groups describing themselves as 'full day care' rose from 200 in 1987 to over 1,000 in 1991 (PPA, 1993). However, some of these groups may in fact appear in the registered day nursery category in official statistics, while others will be the product of the evolution of existing services rather than the opening of new ones.

Part of the decline in local authority day nursery provision, which occurred in England, can be accounted for by some nurseries being converted to family centres. Some of it may also have been due to local authorities switching from direct provision to buying places in the inde-pendent sector; in England, at least, there were fewer children at local authority run playgroups and with salaried child-minders in 1992 than 10 years earlier, as well as fewer children at local authority day nurseries. In contrast, there were increases between 1982 and 1992 in the number of children who local authorities placed and paid for in independent sector services; the increase in Wales was faster than for England, although Wales started from a very low level for day nurseries and child-minders. Even with these increases, the numbers of children involved in 1992 were very small, less than 20,000 in England and less than 1,300 in Wales, in both cases well under 1% of the child population.

Overall, the number of children in publicly funded 'day care' services in England (i.e. in local authority services or placed and paid for by local authorities) increased by 18% between 1982 and 1992, the same growth rate as the under-5s population; by 1992, 1.5% of children under 5 were provided for in this way. In Wales, the number of children in publicly funded 'day care' services nearly doubled between 1982 and 1992. Despite this faster rate of growth, levels of provision in 1992 were still lower than in England, at just over 1% of all children under 5.

Moderate growth occurred between 1982 and 1992 in school provision in England (the figures are not available for Wales to permit comparison).

Reception classes and independent schools achieved 50% growth; maintained nursery education rather less. In fact the growth figures for nursery education, which are for pupils, disguise a slower growth rate – 30% – in the number of places in nursery education. Between 1982 and 1992, the number of full-time pupils in nursery schools and classes fell by over 20%, while the number of part-time pupils grew by over 60%. Growth of pupils in nursery education was therefore enhanced by converting some existing full-time places into part-time provision and by using new places almost entirely on a part-time basis.

Finally, high rates of growth occurred in the supply of provision by child-minders and independent registered nurseries in both England and Wales. In England, provision trebled for private day nurseries, albeit starting from a low level, and more than doubled for child-minding; the growth rates were even higher in Wales. Overall, these two types of day care service accounted for 86% of the growth in day care services in England between 1982–92, and 69% of growth in Wales.

**The use of services**

Tables 2.1a and 2.1b give a good idea of the supply of services, but they are of limited use for assessing the use made of different services by children. For this purpose, we must rely on surveys. In the last 8 years, there have been a number of large-scale national surveys which have asked about use of services. Unfortunately, for reasons outlined below, the data from these surveys are not always comparable, making it impossible to track developments over time; in particular, the surveys illustrate the need for a common and clearly defined classification of services to be agreed and applied routinely.

The General Household Survey (GHS) is a large-scale national study conducted annually for the Government. In 1986, the GHS asked about the attendance of children under 5 at different types of 'education and childcare' services. This showed that 42% of under-5s attended one or other of the services covered. Overall, the most commonly used service was playgroups (accounting for 20% of children) followed by schools (16%), day nurseries (6%) and child-minders (4%). Attendance rose with age: 8% for under-2s, 26% for 2-year-olds, 76% for 3-year-olds, and 89% for 4-year-olds. Playgroups were the most commonly used service for 3-year-olds and schools for 4-year-olds (OPCS, 1988).

Since 1986, there have been some significant developments in services, an increased child population and growing maternal employment as described in Chapter 1. Of the surveys conducted since 1986, some have been concerned exclusively with care arrangements for children while their mothers are at work (Marsh and McKay, 1993; Witherspoon and Prior, 1991). It is a feature of most work in this area that it is assumed that children require care because of maternal employment rather than because of maternal and paternal employment.

The 1991 General Household Survey asked questions about 'childcare for children' which, despite dropping the reference to 'education' found in the 1986 GHS, in fact covers the full range of early childhood services for all children, whether or not their mothers are employed. This survey showed that 65% of children were 'using care' (i.e. education and/or childcare services) in 1991 (OPCS, 1993). Although this appears to show a considerable increase since 1986, the results from the two rounds of the GHS are not comparable due to substantial differences in the classification system used in the 1991 GHS for 'type of service' attended. The 'school/nursery school' category used in 1991 does not distinguish between 'maintained' and 'private' schools as in 1986. More seriously, 'child-minders' are put in with 'nannies' (who do not appear in the 1986 GHS); and all other services are classified according to management and funding rather than type (e.g. 'private or voluntary scheme', 'local authority scheme' or 'workplace facility'), so that for example the 'private or voluntary scheme' category covers both registered nurseries and playgroups. Finally, the 1991 GHS includes a category of 'unpaid family or friends', which accounts for nearly a quarter of all children under 5 but which is missing from the 1986 GHS.

Most recently, in August 1994, results have been published of a survey of children under 8, conducted in 1990 for the Department of Health (Meltzer, 1994). Unfortunately the results cannot be directly compared with those from earlier surveys because of inconsistencies in definitions. Like the 1991 GHS, 'nannies' are included, but unlike the 1991 GHS they are separated out from child-minders. The 1986 GHS has a general category for child-minders, whether registered or not, while the 1990 DoH survey has one category for 'registered child-minder' and another for 'friend or neighbour'. Like the 1991 GHS, the DoH survey includes informal arrangements involving 'fathers' and 'relatives', except that the 1991 GHS includes only 'unpaid' relatives and friends while the DoH survey makes no such stipulation about payment. Most significant is the exclusion from the 1990 survey of 4-year-olds in reception class, and their inclusion in the 1986 and 1991 GHS surveys.

The 1990 Department of Health survey does provide the most up to date and comprehensive information on use of services. According to the survey, *'about half'* of children under 5 used a formal service (excluding reception class). The most common form of provision was playgroups (21%), followed by nursery class or school (15%), then day nursery (8%), friend or neighbour (7%), registered child-minder (6%) and nannies (3%). Use of group services (nurseries, schools, playgroups) increased with age, but provision by individual carers was at similar levels over the age range. In addition to formal services, a substantial number of children were regularly cared for by relatives (27%), mainly grandparents, while 2% were cared for by siblings.

**Features of services**

Amongst the diversity of early childhood services and the statistical complexities, it is still possible to identify a number of features of 'early childhood services' and their use in 1992.

- There is a structural division, both nationally and within most local authorities, between day care services and under-5s education services. In England, schools (maintained and private) provide just over 40% of **places**; day care services just under 60%. In Wales, schools provide just over 50% of places. Although the division for **children attending** is not possible to calculate precisely, the 1986 and 1991 GHS data suggest a 40/60 split, with the majority of children in day care services.

- Under-5s education services are mainly provided and funded publicly; independent schools account for less than 10% of pupils. The situation is reversed for day care services where the great majority of provision is entirely dependent on unsubsidised parental fees. According to the DoH statistics, less than 50,000 children in England have a publicly funded day care place, either in a local authority service or placed and paid for by local authorities, and only 7% of places in day care services are publicly funded in these ways. For Wales, the figures are respectively 1,800 children and 4% of places. These figures may underestimate the **number of children** receiving publicly funded services because they exclude family centres and some children at playgroups and other services whose fees are subsidised from public funds but are not recorded in the official statistics (for example, because a fee subsidy scheme is administered for the local authority by PPA). On the other hand, these figures may overestimate the **proportion of children** receiving publicly funded day care services because the total number of children attending these services is far higher than the places. Even if we adopt generous assumptions (for example, that 5% of children attending playgroup receive some form of fee subsidy), the proportion of children in day care services who are publicly funded still comes to less than 10%.

- Most children attend services – both in day care and schools – for short periods. The most common forms of provision are sessional playgroups (which are open on average for 4.6 sessions per week and are attended by children on average for 2.5 sessions per week) and nursery education (where 89% of children attend on a part-time basis, usually five mornings or five afternoons a week in term time only). According to the 1986 GHS, 76% of children attended services for five-half days or less per week, and nearly half went for three half-days or less. The 1991 GHS, including 'unpaid family and friends' shows a similar picture, with 59% of children receiving 10 hours or less of 'care' per week and a further 22% receiving 11–20 hours.

- Large variations exist in levels of local provision of services, both day care and under-5s education services and both publicly and privately funded (Owen and Moss, 1989).

- A rising proportion of children are attending 'formal' services (i.e. schools, playgroups, nurseries, child-minders), both because there is an increasing supply of education and day care services and because an increasing proportion of children use formal services while their parents are out at work. However, the main forms of care for children while their mothers are at work (and there are no statistics on how children are cared for while fathers are at work) remain informal; fathers, relatives and friends. As Marsh and McKay (1993) note:

*'About a fifth [of working mothers] used child-minders for pre-school children and, in fact, continued to use them during the primary school years. One in ten of 8 and 9 year olds [with employed mothers] are cared for by child-minders. About a third in all [of employed mothers with children under-5] used some kind of nursery, crèche or playgroup and the sudden intervention of nursery schools and playgroups for the 3 and 4 year olds was quite striking: about a quarter of working mothers with 3 and 4 year olds used them probably in combination with other resources [child-minders, partners, parents] to collect them. But even for pre-school children, the most help came from the family: half those [employed mothers] with partners mobilised them for childcare . . . More than a third were helped by their parents and similar numbers of lone parents got help from friends too.' (Marsh and McKay, 1993 p. 365)*

The 1990 Department of Health survey confirms the importance of informal care arrangements; about a quarter of children under 5 were looked after regularly by grandparents or other relatives. Although this arrangement was used by some children with non-employed mothers, 15% of whom had regular care from a relative, it was much

more common (over 40%) for children with employed mothers. Indeed grandparents were the most commonly used child care arrangement for children with mothers who were full-time or part-time employees; in the former case, for example, 38% were cared for regularly by a grandparent and 12% by another relative, compared to 21% using child-minders, 17% playgroups and 14% day nurseries (Meltzer, 1994; Table 4.4).

- The 1991 GHS shows that school attendance is fairly constant across different socio-economic groups, as is the use of 'unpaid family and friends'. However, higher socio-economic groups (professionals, employers and managers, intermediate non-manual workers) are far more likely than other groups to use 'child-minders and nannies', while semi-skilled and unskilled manual workers are much less likely to use 'private or voluntary schemes' (nurseries and playgroups) (Bridgwood and Savage, 1993; Table 7.8).

- The 1990 Department of Health survey also shows considerable differences in the use of services among children from different ethnic groups. 'West Indian or African' children showed high rates of use of registered child-minders, friends or neighbours, nursery education and day nursery, but low attendance at playgroups; care by grandparents was low, but care by other relatives very high. 'Asian or Oriental' children were also low users of playgroups and care by grandparents and high users of nursery education; however, they also showed below-average use of day nurseries, registered child-minders and friends or neighbours (Meltzer, 1994; Table 4.2).

- At least for employed mothers, the costs of using services are regressive. Women with lower earnings pay less for services, but this takes a higher proportion of their earnings (Marsh and McKay, 1993 p. 361, 369).

- Studies of playgroups, which contribute the largest number of places in 'day care', have emphasised that many are poorly resourced, both in terms of income and with respect to the training, pay and conditions of workers, and the standards of accommodation and other material circumstances (Brophy et al., 1992; Statham et al.). There are no recent studies of the resourcing of other types of 'day care' services, in particular child-minding and private day nurseries.

**Summary**    Official statistics on the levels of provision of day care and preschool education need to be read with some caution. However, they reveal in broad terms, the low level of publicly funded day care places, and the high rate of increase in provision in the independent sector in the previous decade; particularly the growth of private day nurseries. Available information on the use of services suggests that a rising proportion of young children are attending 'formal' services of various kinds and this is in part explained by the increase in maternal employment. However, evidence also suggests that large numbers of the children of working mothers rely on 'informal' sources of care including friends and relatives. Finally, it is important to note that attendance at services varies with the age group of children, the area they live in and the employment status and income of their parent or parents.

**Table 2.1a   Places in Day Care Services for children aged 0–7 and in schools for children aged 0–4 England, 1992**

| Type of service | Places (total and as [%] of all children aged 0–4 years) | | Children attending (total and as [%] of all children aged 0–4 years) | |
|---|---|---|---|---|
| **DAY CARE SERVICES** | | | | |
| **Day nurseries** | | | | |
| Local Authority | 23,800 | [0.7%] | 28,400 | [0.9%] |
| Independent | 92,900 | [2.9%] | No information | |
| **Family Centres** | No Information | | No information | |
| **Playgroups** | | | | |
| Local Authority | 1,400 | [*] | 1,600 | [*] |
| Independent | 413,100 | [12.8%] | No information | |
| **Child-minders** | | | | |
| Local Authority | 2,200 | [0.1%] | No information | |
| Independent | 252,100 | [7.8%] | No information | |
| **Out of school clubs + holiday schemes** | | | | |
| Local Authority | 21,700 | | No information | |
| Independent | 37,600 | | No Information | |
| **SCHOOLS†** | | | | |
| **Maintained nursery school and class** | 182,884 | [5.7%] | Full-time =   36,033 [0.1%] Part-time = 293,702 [9.1%] | |
| **Maintained reception class** | 286,688 | [8.6%] | Full-time = 273,400 [8.4%] Part-time =  26,576 [0.8%] | |
| **Independent schools** | 46,384 | [1.4%] | Full-time =   36,334 [1.1%] Part-time =  20,101 [0.6%] | |

* less than 0.05%

†   Places in schools are full-time equivalent places calculated on the basis that two part-time pupils occupy one FTE place.

Sources: Department for Education (1993); Department of Health (1993)

**Table 2.1b   Places in Day Care Services for children aged 0–7 and in schools for children aged 0–4 Wales, 1992**

| Type of service | Places (total and as [%] of all children aged 0–4 years) | | Children attending (total and as [%] of all children aged 0–4 years) | |
|---|---|---|---|---|
| **DAY CARE SERVICES** | | | | |
| **Day nurseries** | | | | |
|    Local Authority | 194 | [0.1%] | 330 | [0.2%] |
|    Independent | 4,599 | [2.4%] | No information | |
| **Family Centres** | No Information | | No information | |
| **Playgroups** | | | | |
|    Local Authority | 263 | [0.1%] | 449 | [0.2%] |
|    Independent | 24,133 | [12.5%] | No information | |
| **Child-minders** | | | | |
|    Local Authority | No information | | No information | |
|    Independent | 10,183 | [5.3%] | No information | |
| **Out of school clubs + holiday schemes** | | | | |
|    Local Authority | No information | | No information | |
|    Independent | No information | | No Information | |
| **SCHOOLS†** | | | | |
| **Maintained nursery school and class** | 18,358 | [9.5%] | Full-time =  7,783 [4.0%] Part-time = 21,150 [11.0%] | |
| **Maintained reception class** | 40,212 | [20.9%] | Full-time = 23,983 [12.5%] Part-time =    433 [0.2%] | |
| **Independent schools** | 936 | [0.5%] | Full-time =    841 [0.4%] Part-time =    189 [0.1%] | |

†   Places in schools are full-time equivalent places calculated on the basis that two part-time pupils occupy one FTE place.

Sources: Welsh Office (1993a, b)

**Table 2.2a   Places in Day Care Services and in schools for children aged 0–4 England, 1982, 1987, 1992**

**No. of Places/children per year**

| | 1982 | 1987 | %change 1982–1987 | 1992 | % change 1987–1992 | % change 1982–1992 |
|---|---|---|---|---|---|---|
| **PUBLIC SECTOR** | | | | | | |
| **Children on registers of facilities provided by local authorities** | | | | | | |
| Day Nurseries | 31,709 | 34,709 | 9.5 | 28,400 | –18.2 | –10.4 |
| Playgroups | 2,715 | 3,370 | 24.1 | 1,600 | –52.5 | –41.1 |
| Child-minders | 2,376 | 1,798 | –24.3 | 2,200 | 22.4 | –7.4 |
| Nursery Education | 235,401 | 276,174 | 17.3 | 329,735 | 19.4 | 40.1 |
| Reception Class | 201,279 | 240,590 | 19.5 | 299,976 | 24.7 | 49.0 |
| **Children placed and paid for by local authorities** | | | | | | |
| Day Nurseries | 1,552 | 1,825 | 17.6 | 2,000 | 9.6 | 28.9 |
| Playgroups | 5,182 | 12,173 | 134.9 | 11,100 | –8.8 | 114.2 |
| Child-minders | 1,908 | 4,984 | 161.2 | 6,300 | 26.4 | 230.2 |
| **INDEPENDENT SECTOR** | | | | | | |
| Day Nurseries* | 21,131 | 30,687 | 45.2 | 91,600 | 198.5 | 333.5 |
| Playgroups* | 366,649 | 404,681 | 10.4 | 409,800 | 1.3 | 11.8 |
| Child-minders* | 96,119 | 148,845 | 54.9 | 252,100 | 69.4 | 162.3 |
| School Pupils | 36,703 | 43,550 | 18.7 | 56,435 | 29.6 | 53.8 |
| **Number of children (thousands)** | | | | | | |
| Under 5 | 2,833 | 3,005 | 6.1 | 3,236 | 7.7 | 14.2 |
| Aged 3 and 4 | 1,078 | 1,182 | 9.6 | 1,286 | 8.8 | 19.3 |

\*   These figures show the number of *places* rather than the number of children: all other figures are for children

Sources:   Department for Education (1993); Department of Education and Science (1992); Department of Health (1983, 1988, 1993b).

**Table 2.2b** Places in Day Care Services and in schools for children aged 0–4 Wales, 1982, 1987, 1992

**No. of Places/children per year**

| | 1982 | 1987 | %change 1982–1987 | 1992 | % change 1987–1992 | % change 1982–1992 |
|---|---|---|---|---|---|---|
| **PUBLIC SECTOR** | | | | | | |
| **Children on registers of facilities provided by local authorities** | | | | | | |
| Day Nurseries | 266 | 391 | 47.0 | 330 | −15.6 | 24.1 |
| Playgroups | 443 | 613 | 38.4 | 449 | −26.8 | −1.4 |
| Primary School | 39,377 | 44,442 | 12.9 | 49,709 | 11.9 | 26.2 |
| Nursery School | 4,120 | 3,999 | −2.9 | 3,640 | −9.0 | −11.9 |
| Nursery Education | † | 26,716 | † | 28,933 | 8.3 | † |
| Reception Class | † | 21,725 | † | 24,416 | 12.4 | † |
| **Children placed and paid for by local authorities** | | | | | | |
| Day Nurseries | 42 | 131 | 211.9 | 238 | 81.7 | 466.7 |
| Playgroups | 247 | 169 | −31.6 | 804 | 374.5 | 224.7 |
| Child-minders | 9 | 61 | 577.8 | 181 | 196.7 | 1,911 |
| **INDEPENDENT SECTOR** | | | | | | |
| Day Nurseries* | 743 | 1,233 | 65.9 | 4,599 | 273.0 | 519.0 |
| Playgroups* | 18,539 | 20,601 | 11.1 | 24,133 | 17.1 | 30.2 |
| Child-minders* | 2,496 | 5,302 | 112.4 | 10,183 | 92.1 | 308.0 |
| School Pupils | 490 | 899 | 83.5 | 1,030 | 14.6 | 110.2 |
| **Number of children (thousands)** | | | | | | |
| Under 5 | 172.3 | 178.9 | 3.8 | 192.3 | 7.5 | 11.6 |
| Aged 3 and 4 | 64.7 | 70.6 | 9.1 | 77.9 | 10.3 | 20.4 |

\* These figures show the number of *places* rather than the number of children: all other figures are for children

† Figures not available.

Sources: Welsh Office (1983, 1988, 1993a, 1993b).

# Coordination

**Introduction**

One of the three functions that the Guidance assigns to Social Services and Education Departments is 'oversight and coordination'. By making the review of day care provision a shared responsibility, the Act places particular emphasis on the relationship between Social Services and Education. In their approach to coordination, the Act and Guidance build on long-standing policy. In the 1970s the Department of Health and Social Security (DHSS) and Department of Education and Science (DES) issued two Guidance circulars on under-5s services advocating greater coordination between statutory (Social Services, Education and Health) and voluntary agencies (LASSL (76)5 and LASSL (78)1). The model envisaged in the Act and Guidance involves separate day care and education service systems for young children, located in separate, but collaborating, conceptual, administrative and legislative frameworks.

This chapter is particularly concerned with the relationship between Social Services and Education Departments in relation to day care and education provision for young children. However, the Guidance also stresses the need for Social Services Departments 'to have regard' to links with local authority departments beyond Education, with other statutory authorities, such as health authorities and National Health Service (NHS) Trusts, and links with local voluntary organisations, community groups, minority ethnic interest groups, the private child care sector and employers (Guidance, para. 4.7).

Within this broad range of potential relationships, this chapter looks at coordination between Social Services and other agencies under two broad headings: structures for coordination; and the extent of coordination between agencies in the implementation process, both in general and for specific aspects such as the review process. Coordination in Wales is discussed separately, later in the chapter.

**Structures for coordination**

For many years it has been recognised that a more coordinated approach to services for young children needs to be supported by appropriate structures, although these by themselves do not guarantee coordination. The 1976 Circular concentrated on machinery for coordination. The 1978 Circular encouraged local authorities which had not already done so to set up structures for interdepartmental coordination in service provision, such as joint under-5s liaison groups, and to establish or improve collaboration with the voluntary sector.

The Children Act returns to the need for closer collaboration between departments with the Guidance stating that local authorities

*'acting as corporate bodies should decide on the mechanism for ensuring that all relevant departments contribute actively to policy development on services for young children'* (Guidance, para. 4.4).

A number of possible mechanisms are suggested but, as with the earlier Circulars, the Guidance offers no ideal model, favouring local diversity and discretion.

In the sample English authorities, one had gone beyond coordination between departments to the integration of all under-5s services into one department (Education). Two local authorities, while not taking this major step, had made substantive organisational changes to promote interdepartmental coordination, establishing early years units located in administrative or chief executive's offices (both backed by a committee or subcommittee). There were no other jointly funded or interdepartmental posts, although in a few cases there were departmental posts intended to promote coordination, for example, a Day Care Review Adviser in one Social Services Department, and an Early Years Coordinator in an Education Department.

Eight local authorities (including the two mentioned above who had initiated substantive organisational change) had other coordinating structures primarily intended to promote interdepartmental working. All eight had some form of member group: four subcommittees, one committee, one early years group and two advisory committees. One of these authorities also had an officer group on early years strategy.

Membership always included representation from Social Services and Education, supplemented in four authorities by representation from other local authority departments; in two cases from the voluntary sector; and in one case from Health and a TEC. The most broad-based group, an early years subcommittee, included representatives from four local authority departments (including Equal Opportunities and Economic Development), as well as from Health, the TEC and the voluntary and private sectors.

A second type of coordinating structure was concerned primarily to promote communication and collaboration between non-statutory agencies and/or between non-statutory agencies and the local authority. Nine authorities had a forum, liaison committee or other structure at local authority level specifically concerned with services for children under 8 and involving voluntary and private organisations with, in most cases, some local authority representation. A further eight reported district forums or liaison groups, covering part or all of the local authority. Altogether 13 authorities reported this type of structure at local authority or district level or both.

Most authorities (14 out of 18), therefore, reported some type of coordinating structure concerned primarily or wholly with under-8s services. Most structures (25 out of 28) predated implementation of the Act, although the review was stimulating some further developments: two interdepartmental member groups were continuations of groups established for the review, and some reviews had flagged up the need for new coordinating structures in their conclusions.

Overall, however, coordinating structures remained patchy, both in type and coverage. Most were primarily intended to provide opportunities for exchange and discussion, and in some cases for consultation and advice, rather than being means for developing a coordinated approach to the development of policy and the deployment of resources. Nor was the existence of structures a guarantee of effective coordination. One interdepartmental members group was not very successful because, in the view of an officer, old rivalries continued; the chair of a subcommittee observed that there was still a complete lack of integration between Social Services and Education; an under-8s advisory group met infrequently and carried little influence; a multi-agency group to implement the Children Act was ineffective and eventually disbanded. Effective coordination might well occur in the absence of or despite structures due to good working relationships between individual officers.

**Implementing the Act**

The Guidance recommends that:

> 'the Act requires a corporate local authority policy on implementation that will cover all the issues including those which require collaboration and corporate planning . . . The Act is directed at the local authority as a whole and cannot succeed without effective inter-departmental collaboration at all levels' (Guidance, para. 1.8).

In England, in the 17 authorities for which information was available, the implementation of the Act was most commonly led by a group in Social Services, sometimes supplemented by working groups on specific issues that included representatives from other departments or agencies. Only four authorities established an interdepartmental structure to oversee the whole Act: a Children Act Steering Group (Social Services, Education and Health), a Children Act Working Team (Social Services, Education, Leisure, Housing, Economic Development, Health and a voluntary agency) and two corporate groups consisting of high level officers from key departments.

Within this general approach to implementation, local authorities varied in how they tackled under-8s services. Seven local authorities established subgroups specifically concerned with the implementation of under-8s issues in the Act. Usually these included at least one representative from outside Social Services, although membership was never broad enough to include all or most interested constituencies. Most authorities (11 out of 18) did not establish a specialist structure. In one case, an authority with a corporate structure for implementation specifically allocated different tasks on under-8s services to different departments through that structure. In other cases, the task of implementation was passed to a specific officer or officers within Social Services or Education.

**Common policies**    The Guidance emphasises that local authorities as a whole should have policies on support services for children in need, as well as for day care and preschool education, agreed by *'all relevant departments and organisations'* who should also be involved in the process of development (Guidance, para. 1.8). Neither had yet happened frequently in practice. As Chapter 4 describes in more detail, only three authorities adopted 'extensive inter-agency debate' in drawing up a children in need policy. Mostly policies were developed within Social Services.

No authority had developed common policies on children in need, covering criteria for identification and admission to services applied across all agencies. One authority produced a common broad statement of principles, but this had not led to common interdepartmental policies. The other authorities had not even agreed broad principles. In two authorities, the development of a local authority definition had been recommended (in one case by consultants, in the other by the review), and two more had attempted but already failed to achieve corporate definitions. (See Chapter 4 for further discussion on definitions of children in need.)

Only three authorities had an agreed policy on under-8s services. In one case, this was part of the process of integrating all services into Education, while in a second case, strategic aims had been agreed by an under-8s unit and committee already in place which provided a strong mechanism for coordination. Neither owed anything to the Children Act. In the third case, however, an Early Years Strategy had recently been ratified. While this came out of a pre-Children Act history of interest in a common approach, the Act itself was seen as 'forcing the timing' of this development.

**The review**   The duty to review day care services falls jointly on Social Services and Education. The Guidance stresses the need for wider participation to include district councils, other statutory bodies, voluntary organisations, the private sector, employers and parents. A further study on the specific issue of the review is being undertaken by the Early Childhood Unit at the National Children's Bureau for the DoH which will provide a fuller picture of the review process in different authorities.

*Preparing the review*

All but one of the English authorities had completed first drafts of their reviews at the time of the fieldwork (although these included one authority where a draft had been prepared but rejected by members). The most common arrangement for preparing the review (eight authorities) was a joint exercise involving Social Services and Education officers, although input was not necessarily equal. In four authorities, the working team preparing the review included members from other agencies. In one case, for example, the review team included officers from Health, a voluntary organisation and the local Race Equality Council, as well as officers from the two main providing departments.

In one of the remaining six authorities, the preparatory work and initial drafting had been contracted out to an outside body, while in the other five the review had been prepared essentially by one officer. In three cases, however, this was because of particular local circumstances: the creation of a post of Review Adviser in one Social Services Department; the integration of all services into Education in another authority; and the presence of an officer in an Early Years Unit in a third authority.

Beyond the team or individual preparing the review, most authorities (14 out of 18) had steering groups to oversee the work. Three authorities delegated this task to existing coordinating bodies. The rest was fairly evenly divided between those which had steering groups drawn exclusively from within the local authority (six authorities) and those which had groups with representatives from outside which included Health, TECs, the private and voluntary sector and district councils (five authorities). Only a third involved elected members on steering groups. This reflected the mostly marginal role of members in the implementation of the Act.

Three authorities appeared not to have consulted other organisations either before or after preparing a draft report (although one of these authorities had recently undertaken a large consultation exercise when preparing an integrated under-5s policy, and felt there was no need to undertake a second exercise). Seven mentioned some form of consultation during drafting; four, consultation afterwards; and four, consultation both before and afterwards. The most common form of consultation (8 out of 18) consisted of a survey or questionnaire to groups of parents or providers or both; otherwise consultation usually involved seeking the views of various organisations (sometimes through existing structures like forums) and, in three cases, organising public meetings.

Consultation with ethnic minorities was not widespread, and when attempted was generally acknowledged to be unsuccessful. This issue is discussed further in Chapter 6.

*Content and recommendations*

A recent study of reviews in one region of England concluded that '*the majority of reports were primarily descriptive rather than analytical*' (Trinder, 1993, p. 48). This was also true of our national sample. Reports varied greatly in length, but most space was allotted to describing services, policies and other features of the authorities' approach. Five of the sixteen authorities with draft or final reviews had a section explicitly titled 'issues'; other headings used by different authorities included 'local needs', 'matters which cause concern' and 'progress and development' which identified some areas where further work was felt to be needed.

However, other authorities raised issues in sections entitled 'recommendations' or 'action plans'. Altogether nine of the sixteen authorities had specific recommendations, while a tenth had a short section entitled 'The Way Forward: Joint Tasks for Education and Social Services'. In three cases, 'issues' and 'recommendations' were integrated into one section, while two authorities discussed 'issues' but provided no 'recommendations'.

Like Trinder, in her regional study, our national sample revealed few examples of measurable targets, timetables or costings: only three authorities included timings for some or all of their proposals and only one included any estimates of cost. This reflects wide variation in how specific the proposals were, ranging from reviews whose proposals were vague in the extreme to two local authorities which had a list of specific proposals, each of which was timetabled for completion. Examples from two reviews both dealing with coordination, illustrate this variability:

*'The development of a collaborative approach between Local Authority departments and the voluntary and private sectors will help to ensure quality services for young children.'*

*'Officers from Education and Social Services should explore further the "coordinating framework building on existing structures" described [earlier in the review] and with the voluntary/private sector and ethnic minority interests: recommend the preferred model; provide an implementation plan. Completion Date: December 1993.'*

All ten authorities whose reviews contained recommendations included references to coordination. Five referred to the need for corporate or inter-agency policies or strategies, either about services more generally – 'services for young children', 'day care services' – or in relation to specific services or groups of children, in particular disabled and other children in need. Nine authorities put forward the need for better coordinating structures. These ranged from expressing very general objectives (*'a model for planning and development on an inter-agency basis should be devised'*), through suggesting the strengthening of existing structures (*'the Under 5s Forum could be strengthened to fulfil this coordination role'*) to proposing a specific new structure (*'the Director of Social Services and the Chief Education Officer should establish a Strategic Planning Group for under-8s provision'*). Finally, six reviews recommended inter-agency coordination on specific topics, mainly concerning training and other support activities.

**Comparisons with Wales**

The situation in Wales differed in three key ways from that in England, mainly due to initiatives adopted by the Welsh Office. First, the Social Services Inspectorate (SSI) encouraged all eight authorities to adopt a multi-agency approach to implementation, especially on the issue of children in need. All authorities had, at least, a multi-agency group on children in need (although none had, at the time of fieldwork, produced an interdepartmental policy). Five went further and had a multi-agency implementation group, including not only key local authority departments but also other statutory and voluntary agencies; this was usually supplemented by a group in Social Services concerned specifically with that Department's implementation strategy.

Second, by early 1992, while the extent of coordinating structures specifically concerned with services for children under 8 was similar in England and Wales (with the exception that no Welsh authorities had made substantive organisational changes to promote coordination), Wales had made more progress on another front, again in part in response to Welsh

Office encouragement. Six out of eight Welsh authorities had a Joint Planning Group for Children's Services, a broad structure concerned with all services for children up to the age of 16, and within which day care and related services might also be discussed. Alongside these groups, forums involving voluntary and private organisations were being developed for children and families in general.

Finally, only two Welsh authorities had drafted their reviews at the time of the fieldwork; one had not even begun the process, intending instead to develop district reviews in preparation for local government reorganisation.

Factors impeding coordination

A number of factors were widely commented on during interviews as impeding coordination. One major constraint was the different philosophical underpinnings to the approach and objectives of different departments, especially Social Services and Education. Without shared concepts and objectives, shared policies are hard to achieve. As one officer in Education said of the attempt to agree a corporate definition of need:

> *'Philosophically and intellectually it is impossible to accept a definition of "in need" and agree priorities when we are providing a universal service . . . We will not choose children deemed to be needy.'*

A second problem frequently mentioned was the impact of other legislation and reforms. Other agencies, especially Education and Health, often appeared too preoccupied by the demands made on them by these changes to have sufficient time and interest to spare for the Children Act. Some officers in these agencies saw the Act as mainly Social Services' affair, of secondary importance both in absolute terms and in the context of the other demands on their time. A senior officer in an Education Department, recently thrown into crisis by devolution of budgets, the redundancy of 16 advisers and the resignation of senior officers, observed that:

> *'The Children Act affected Welfare Officers but not the rest of Education. If the Children Act were the only thing around, then there might have been greater awareness. But the Education Reform Act came on stream at the same time and most of our work was geared towards that . . . Everyone can see the benefits of joint working but you have to prioritise, and our main concern is with the curriculum.'*

The maelstrom of change also made it harder, in some cases, for officers in Social Services to identify the right people to work with in Education and

Health. Others saw the reforms as working against each other. In particular, the increased autonomy of schools was seen as being at odds with the adoption of a coordinated approach across services and the duty for local authorities to provide for children in need.

In at least six English authorities, the attempt to develop a coordinated approach was undermined by the development of strategies to promote child care for working parents as part of an economic development or equal opportunities programme. Located outside Social Services or Education, such programmes had little contact with other parts of the local authority concerned with early childhood services.

Finally, coordination requires commitment, skill and resources, all applied consistently over time. A pervasive problem with the review was the lack of resources available, which hindered every stage of the exercise, not least attempting to consult with the wide range of groups and individuals proposed in the Guidance. Only four authorities mentioned 'dedicated' additional resources made available for the exercise; most relied on existing staff taking on extra work. Where, in addition, there were not well-established and regularly used channels and processes for consultation (as was the case, for example, with ethnic minorities) either little happened or what did happen was unsuccessful.

**Summary**

The early stages of implementing the Children Act have created new opportunities for inter-agency collaboration and coordination. The review was widely seen as being one such opportunity. However, there are a number of structural factors limiting the exploitation of these opportunities.

Coordination is, in fact, a generic label for a variety of possibilities: exchange of information and discussion; consultation; working together on a common task; and developing a common approach to services involving planning, resources and policy, which eventually may involve the integration of responsibilities or services. Each possibility requires particular conditions in which to flourish. Broadly speaking, exchange, discussion and consultation were the most common forms of coordination found in the local authorities studied, although even this was by no means universal. Working together on a common task (except for the review) and developing a common approach to under-8s services were less frequent. There was, therefore, very limited progress on common policies, and slow progress in other areas, for example, in establishing and operating a joint register for children with disabilities (see Chapter 4).

# Provision

**Introduction**     Care and education services for young children have evolved separately in Britain, and the Children Act largely reflects a concern with day care services. In this area, the aim of the Act is that public responsibility for the provision of day care for children in need is seen as one of a range of family support services available to those in need of them. For other children, day care continues to be a private arrangement between parents and providers, although the local authority has a regulatory role and may also exercise a power to provide for children not in need.

The definition of children 'in need' was a new and critical feature in determining which children had access to services provided by the public purse. Part III, Section 17(1) of the Act places a 'general duty' on local authorities to *'safeguard and promote the welfare of children within their area who are in need'*, and to promote the *'upbringing of such children by their families'* by providing a range and level of services appropriate to those children's needs. Section 17(10) details the parameters of 'in need'. There are three categories:

- a child who is *'unlikely to achieve or maintain, or have the opportunity of maintaining, a reasonable standard of health or development without the provision'* of services

- a child whose *'health or development is likely to be significantly impaired, or further impaired, without the provision'*

- a child who is *'disabled'*.

This was the first time children with disabilities were to be provided for within children's legislation, and this represented a significant step on the route to recognising them as *'children first then as persons with a disability'* (Guidance, para. 1.3).

The duty to provide for children in need is a general one in that local authorities *'are not expected to meet every individual need but to make decisions about priorities and make general provision on the basis of that need'* (Guidance, para. 2.11). As well as a duty to provide day care services for children in need, local authorities are given a power to provide day care services for children not in need, but the suggested circumstances in which they might do this are limited (Guidance, para. 4.8).

Arising from this part of the Act, local authorities also have a duty to identify the extent of need within their area, to publish information about the services available for users, to aid the identification of children in need and to keep a register of children with disabilities separately from that held by health authorities.

This chapter examines the implementation of the sections of the Act concerned with the provision of services.

**Definitions of 'in need'**

Findings from the first stage of our study show that the interpretation of the duty to define 'in need' varied widely. This variation in part reflected existing diversity across England and Wales in expenditure on, and local interest in, early childhood services. It also reflected the financial difficulties many local authorities were facing at the time of implementation. Definitions of children 'in need', however, were intended to be located in the legislation: that is, they should be needs-led and should reflect the broad spirit of the Act, rather than be resource-led.

Multi-agency and cross-departmental participation in drawing up a children in need policy was encouraged by the requirement under Section 27 of the Act to work together for children in need, and reflected a general concern with partnership and coordination in the Act which is discussed further in Chapter 3. Despite this, a multi-agency or interdepartmental approach to defining children in need was found in only three English authorities. Wales was generally more successful at cross-departmental and multi-agency policy-making in this area, which may be explained by the encouragement of such an approach by the Welsh SSI (see Chapter 3), with six of the Welsh authorities approaching the definition of in need through 'extensive inter-agency debate'.

The second approach, adopted by eight of the English authorities, was to make use of Children Act implementation subgroups located in Social Services Departments. The third approach was for one or two officers from Social Services to draw up the definition, and distribute draft policies to colleagues for comment. Five English and two Welsh authorities adopted this approach.

While a multi-agency approach to defining need was not common among English authorities, even where this was the case it did not necessarily result in common policies between departments. None of the authorities had yet achieved definitions of need which applied beyond Social Services Departments.

Two English authorities had not drawn up a policy at all on the basis that the principle of dividing children according to an 'in need' criteria conflicted with their attempts to provide more universally available services.

Within broad definitions of need, fourteen English and three Welsh authorities prioritised those children who were already members of a defined group, such as those listed on the Child Protection Register or subject to a court order. Twelve English and seven Welsh authorities either had a general clause or relied totally on local assessments to decide whether a child was 'in need'. Some local authorities, therefore, included both previously defined groups and general indicators in their definition of need. One northern county council, for example, put *'children in need of protection from abuse'* at the top of their list, and ended with *'children who are otherwise disadvantaged through deprivation and/or discrimination'*. The effect of such combination of objectives was to prioritise statutory responsibilities over more general need, but simultaneously to permit local officers discretionary powers of advocacy for a particular child.

There was less general agreement on the role of socioeconomic indicators in the definition of 'in need'. Perhaps wary of the potential demand for day care, only eight English and three Welsh authorities recognised poverty as a contributory factor to the definition of 'in need'. Of these, one English and two Welsh authorities understood poverty to be an indicator of general need in a geographical area or neighbourhood, and seven English and one Welsh authority listed poverty or severe financial hardship as one of a list of indicators for assessing individual need. One of these local authorities used poverty in conjunction with a *'cluster of social factors'*, such as *'poor or temporary housing, violent relationships, social isolation'*.

While the White Paper preceding the Children Act and the Guidance appeared to support a broad approach to the provision of services, the use of the term 'in need' in the legislation, and the general financial pressures on local authorities, seemed to encourage the principle of targeting resources on specific groups of children. Tension between the two approaches to service delivery was apparent in our study in both use of the principle of targeting and in strategies to effect actual change in the client group served by the policy. In our sample, the explicit principle of targeting was often seen as extending the principle of 'greatest need' to a stigmatising degree. Only six English and three Welsh authorities stated that their intention was to target resources, or restrict access, in this way.

At the time of our interviews in late 1992/early 1993, it appeared that few authorities had changed or intended to change their existing methods of assessing need or priority for access to day care services. There had been no change in assessment methods in thirteen English or any of the eight Welsh authorities. Five English local authorities, however, had already implemented new policies on children in need; two had comprehensive and county-wide assessment forms; one had drawn up a very limited definition of need, leaving little room for professional discretion; a fourth had a complex prioritising system accompanied by training of officers completing assessments. In this authority implementation had coincided with local reorganisation and reorientation of Social Services. The fifth local authority had very explicit 'targeting' with clear and restrictive criteria for access to services according to three levels of need. One Welsh local authority had undergone a partial change in assessment procedure. This was the establishment of multi-disciplinary Family Resource Teams for all children, including those with disabilities.

It appeared that most of the effort had gone into debating the issues and creating the policy, rather than putting it into practice at this stage. Local authorities were reluctant to adopt an entirely mechanistic approach to assessment, preferring to value professional judgement and recognising the infinite variety of potential situations of need.

**Identifying the extent of need**

While the duty to define need was largely an extension of existing Social Services practice, the duty to identify the extent of need in an authority was entirely new. Evidence from the study suggests that it had proved difficult for local authorities to complete at the time of our fieldwork. Eight English and five Welsh authorities, for example, had made no attempt to identify the extent of need. The reasons given for this were that it had a low priority in the first year of implementation, that information systems were often inadequate and/or incompatible and that research facilities were unavailable. Of the other local authorities, none believed they had reached a satisfactory assessment of the extent of need in the community.

Some of the ways in which local authorities had approached the task of identifying need included: using the model provided by Community Care Plans and adapting it to children's services; adopting a multi-agency approach by defining a range of indicators in Health, Education and Social Services that fed into a central internal information system; and identifying sources of relevant data such as existing clients, clients of other departments, and more general deprivation indicators. The most limited attempt at defining need involved estimating an authority's 'needy' children from names on the child protection register and health authority disability register, on which basis the authority arrived at an estimated total number of 600 children.

Other examples of information-gathering were related to the duty to identify the scale of need. These included: a monitoring group for children in need; a regular audit of language needs across the authority; and grant-aiding a children's information service to monitor enquiries and provide data for the next review. One local authority had been conducting a strategic review of children's services and had interviewed children about their perceptions of services during the course of this, which enabled user-data to be collected. Developing information systems that fulfilled the strategic planning role was seen as an important next step in many authorities, and tied in well with the triennial review duty.

**Children with disabilities**

The Guidance states that local authorities' efforts to keep accurate and comprehensive disability registers should *'help ensure that children with disabilities gain access to services for which the Act makes provision'* (Guidance, para. 2.19). The implementation of this duty, however, had proved equally as difficult for local authorities as identifying the extent of need. For example, none of the sample authorities had an operating joint register at the time of the fieldwork. Two Welsh and six English local authorities had proposals in hand for the development of such registers with Health and Education Departments, and in others more informal discussions were taking place to address the task. In one outer London borough, a joint Social Services/health authority questionnaire had been distributed to collect data on users' and carers' needs.

Some of the comments about this duty to ensure access to services for children with disabilities illuminated the problem:

*'a long neglected area in co-ordination'*

*'[demonstrates] a lack of coherence in policies'*

*'an absolute nightmare for planning'*

*'Children with special needs receive services from a diverse range of providers. [This provision] needs to be better coordinated, with information more systematically available.'*

*'[It will cause] serious problems in coordination exacerbated by the proliferation of competing NHS Trust units'*

*'There is no formal mechanism for health authorities to relay information on numbers and types of disability to providing departments.'*

These comments echo some of the more general constraints on coordination between agencies discussed in Chapter 3.

While there was some evidence that general awareness of the needs of children with disabilities for under-8s services had been raised by the Act, at the time of our interviews the Children Act had made little impact on services for children with disabilities. At most there had been some reorganisation of the location of services to reflect the 'child-first, disability-second' philosophy, and some additional monies made available for sponsored places in child-minding and playgroups.

**Range of services**  There are various ways in which a local authority can provide day care services. They can make direct provision through their own day nurseries or family centres, with places most usually reserved for children in need. They can also support/grant-aid services in the community, such as playgroups. In addition they can sponsor individual children in need to attend day care services in the independent sector, using services offered by child-minders, playgroups and, in some cases, private nurseries. The levels of provision of day care, and the balance between local authority provision and services provided by the independent sector, vary greatly between local authority areas, as does the extent to which local authorities financially support community-based services or purchase places in other sectors. Thus, each local authority in the sample was starting from a different position in terms of level and type of provision of day care.

In our sample, thirteen English and four Welsh local authorities ran their own day nurseries or playgroups. Thirteen English and six Welsh local authorities had, or were planning, family centres. In five English and five Welsh areas national voluntary organisations were involved in providing or planning these family centres. Three English and one Welsh local authorities had combined centres that offered care and education to make available a range of activities for children and families within single centres, often run jointly by two local authority departments.

All the sample authorities offered paid places with child-minders for children in need. In four Welsh and six English authorities (all but one of the latter were metropolitan boroughs), retainer fees, enhanced rates or additional specialised training were available to some child-minders to encourage them to offer care to specific children. A few authorities were developing this scheme to offer a service to children with disabilities. Twelve English authorities, and seven Welsh local authorities sponsored places in playgroups. There was some extension of this to children with disabilities.

All the Welsh local authorities operated a Special Needs Referral Scheme funded by the All Wales Mental Handicap Strategy, and in some cases this had been extended to children with other disabilities.

Finally, four English and six Welsh authorities had a few places available to children in need to attend private or voluntary day nurseries. This was achieved through direct sponsorship, through purchase of places, or, in one instance, through a condition of planning permission.

The impression of the position for grant aid to both child-minders and playgroups is that the overall level of financial support offered is low, ranging from no support at all to fairly substantial grants to individuals and groups (in some, usually metropolitan, areas). This echoes the findings of Statham et al. (1990), who concluded that *'with a few exceptions, the level of financial support for playgroups from public funds was extremely low'* (p. 89).

The remaining eight service types, ranging from out-of-school facilities to toy libraries and playbuses, are family support services rather than day care, and are not the focus of this study. In general, local authorities tended to be only marginally involved in supporting provision through grant-aiding which was dependent on the local profile of early years work. Two metropolitan areas had play resource centres which supported the voluntary organisations, but those centres, while valued, were considered to be vulnerable to cuts in local authority budgets at the time of interview. Central government financial support for inner cities was undergoing a process of change from small scale Urban Aid grants to City Challenge at the time of our fieldwork. This was having the effect of closing child care projects in areas no longer supported by Urban Aid and opening up possibilities in those areas awarded City Challenge monies. Other avenues for developing child care resources were being sought through TECs. These were generally in a planning stage at the time of our visits.

Gathering financial data in local authorities is, however, difficult. For children in need, there are difficulties involved in assessing the level of resources devoted to sponsorship of places, whether directly, through Section 17 budgets, or indirectly, through grant-aiding local groups. Budgets were often not compiled in a manner amenable to this analysis. Nor has there been any evaluation of the accuracy of figures published by the DoH from returns by local authorities. We are reliant on the comments of local authority officers who reported their budgets to be insufficient in this area, and that generally both the availability of suitable service providers for children in need and the availability of monies to pay them formed a small proportion of the perceived need for the service. In short, it appeared that there was little extra expenditure on provision evident in the first year of implementation, with the majority of extra resources having been spent on regulation.

**Review recommendations**    Eight authorities had recommendations in their review documents that related to provision. All eight referred to the need for more or better provision for certain groups of children, most commonly disabled and other children 'in need', but also under-2s, school-age children and, in one case, the need for developing models of full day care for rural areas. Four authorities referred to the need to allocate or target resources more specifically for children in need or particular areas.

No authorities made any recommendations concerning provision for the whole range of children not in need, although one authority at least already had *'a policy position on aiming to provide universal service with the opportunity for everyone to have equal access to services'*. Five authorities, however, raised the issue of access to services by low income families, although only one review contained a specific recommendation for action in this respect.

**Summary**    Local authorities had a wide range of family support services, but those available to children in need tended to be restricted to either sessional or full day care, and did not include educational facilities. A range of services, however, is not the same as a choice of available services for the user, whether designated as 'in need' or not. For children not in need, the trends in early childhood services discussed in Chapter 2 suggest there is a growth in part-time places, and in full day care in the private sector, although regional variations in level of provision persist. The question of the affordability of day care is not an issue discussed in the Act or in the Guidance, despite some attention to other parameters of diversity.

In conclusion, if the aim of the Children Act was to draw the public provision of day care more firmly into a welfare model of public services, then it both continues a national tradition and it has been more or less successful. Local authorities have approached the Children Act from within a welfare perspective but also within the context of diminishing public funds. The direction taken, therefore, has been towards a more selective rather than a less selective approach to day care. There has been some resistance to this, particularly in local authorities which have taken an active role in encouraging day care as a tool to promote education and employment.

# Regulation and Support

**Introduction**

The introduction of a new 'modernised registration system' was one of the most far-reaching aspects of the Act in relation to early years services. The new regulatory framework introduced by the Act extended local authorities' duties and powers beyond a limited group of children in need to large numbers of children in a range of day care settings. Although day care services had been regulated since the late forties, the new provisions of the Act and Guidance were welcomed in day care circles, as previous legislation, the 1948 Nurseries and Child-minders Regulation Act, had been criticised for being difficult to enforce and unevenly implemented between areas (Elfer and Beasely, 1991).

The aims of the new system as outlined in paragraph 4.9 of the Guidance were to: protect children; provide reassurance to parents; *ensure services meet acceptable standards and ensure an agreed framework for the provision of services'*. To this end, the law specified a set of mandatory requirements, relating to numbers of children, staff:child ratios, health and safety of premises and equipment, maintenance of records and notification of changes in staff, to vary across a range of settings (Guidance, para. 7.38). The Act included services providing out-of-school care for children aged between 5 and 8 in the new registration system, and introduced annual inspection of services. The Guidance also contains general advice to local authorities about less tangible issues relating to good practice and the principles underpinning quality of care in children's services. It is implied that the use of both the mandatory requirements and the discretionary powers invested in local authorities, as well as ensuring *'acceptable standards'*, can also fulfil the objective of *'providing a framework for good quality care'* (Guidance, para. 7.44). Regulating to improve the quality of services inevitably raises issues about the need for training, advice and support of various kinds to providers. While the Act recognises the need for support, it gives local authorities a power, rather than a duty to provide it (Guidance, para. 3.34).

A subsequent circular from the Department of Health (LAC 1/93) was issued in response to concern that some local authorities had been approaching the task of regulation 'over-zealously'. It states that local authorities should not apply the Guidance rigidly, that the Guidance does not have the force of law and that authorities should adopt an approach which is sufficiently *'encouraging and flexible'* to encourage expansion of services as a primary goal. The advice in the Circular has been taken by some to represent a dilution of the standards originally proposed in the Act (Elfer, 1993). In addition, a recent case in the family proceedings court, recently upheld in the high court, challenged a local authority's powers to enforce a 'no smacking policy' on a child-minder in the face of parental opposition. This has appeared to undermine further the status of aspects of the Guidance and left local authorities in some doubt as to their exact role in the regulation function in relation to such good practice issues.

In the year following implementation local authorities had a number of tasks to complete in setting up a new registration system: they had to devise criteria for registration with other departments within the authority and outside agencies; they had to set up new structures and procedures for the registration and inspection process; and they had to re-register existing provision within a year. These tasks were to be completed in addition to dealing with new applicants.

This chapter presents a summary of the findings as they relate to how the local authorities in the study had approached regulation and the associated support functions in the first year of implementation.

**Organisation and staffing**

The implementation of the new provisions on regulation had, for many authorities, entailed a reorganisation of their previous arrangements for registration and inspection. In just over half (10 out of 18) of the English authorities, this had involved giving responsibility for regulation to independent inspection units although, in two of these, child-minders continued to be regulated by the main providing department. Two of the English authorities with independent inspection units employed a generic approach to inspection, with inspectors having both children's and adults' services among their caseloads. Other authorities had retained children's services as a specialism.

In Wales, only two authorities had opted for inspection units, although a further two were considering such a move. The move to independent inspection in these authorities generally reflected a split between regulation and support. In the remaining eight English and six Welsh authorities which had kept regulation within the providing department, the need for provision of support as part of the regulation process was offered as a rationale for not placing registration and inspection at 'arm's length' from the rest of the department.

**Table 5.1  The organisation and staffing of regulation in example local authorities**

| Local Authority | Responsibility for registration and inspection | Department | Staffing level (N) | Support role Present | Provision type | Number of places (N)[1] |
|---|---|---|---|---|---|---|
| **A (Inner London borough)** | Under-8s social workers (for child-minders) | Children and families division of SSD | 7 social workers; 4 temporary staff | Yes | CM | 485 |
| | Generic inspectors (for other day care) | Inspection unit | 3 Inspectors who also inspect adult services | No | PG | 32 |
| | | | | | DN | 24 |
| **B (Metropolitan council)** | Day care officers | Quality assurance unit | 4 | No | CM | 504 |
| | | | | | PG | 84 |
| | | | | | DN | 52 |
| **C (County council)** | Day care advisers | Area offices | 16 | Yes | CM | 2,010 |
| | | | | | PG | 353 |
| | | | | | DN | 25 |
| **D (Outer London borough)** | Under-8s advisers | Social work teams | 12 | Yes | CM | 759 |
| | | | | | PG | 87 |
| | | | | | DN | 2 |
| **E (Welsh county)** | Inspectors | Service evaluation unit | 1 | Yes | CM | 218 |
| | | | | | PG | 68 |
| | | | | | DN | 9 |

KEY: CM = child-minder; DN = day nursery; PG = playgroup

1.  Source for provision: DoH returns, 1991 (Figures exclude 'supervised activities' and out-of-school provision.)

Extra resources had been found for regulation in most local authorities. They included new posts, regrading of existing staff and the employment of temporary staff to cover the re-registration period. Overall, this extra funding found for regulation accounted for the largest part of any additional resources gained for under 8s as a consequence of the Children Act. However, there was a large amount of variation across all of the local authorities in staffing levels in relation to workload. Table 5.1 illustrates some of this variation.

Few authorities had developed any concept of *'appropriate workload'* as recommended in the Guidance (para. 7.21). There was a widespread perception among staff involved in registration and inspection that their tasks remained under-resourced and, in some authorities, under-graded in relation to other inspectors. Some staff said that they had not received adequate training either in inspection skills or child development to prepare them for their new role.

**Developing the guidelines/ standards**

The Guidance recommended a participatory approach to developing the registration guidelines involving *'all relevant departments in the local authority'* (Guidance, paras 7.3, 7.5). This reflected the more general emphasis on coordination which is discussed in Chapter 3. Two broad approaches were apparent among the authorities included in the study. The first was for staff involved in registration and inspection to draw up documents which were then sent out for comment to a variety of other agencies including Health, Education, voluntary and private providers. The second approach was more participatory and involved setting up working groups, which included other departments and agencies, to draw up the regulation guidelines. In general, there had been minimal involvement from departments outside Social Services. Drawing up guidelines for services for children aged between 5 and 8 was more likely to involve a collaborative approach including Leisure and Recreation or other relevant authority departments as well as providers. At this relatively early stage of implementation, only one authority provided examples of joint inspection visits by Social Services and Education and had a long-term aim of covering a proportion of services in this way.

Attempts to involve outside agencies such as voluntary groups or providers varied among authorities. Those who adopted a very consultative approach to the development of the guidelines believed this to have been a key to successful implementation and keeping providers 'on board' in what might otherwise have appeared a threatening exercise. The response of providers is discussed more fully later in this chapter.

**Implementing standards**

Very few alterations or other additional requirements were made by authorities to the standards as recommended in the Guidance. Some authorities had made slight amendments to staff:child ratios in certain age ranges: most notably for babies in full day care (as is suggested by the Guidance itself) or for children aged between 2.5 and 3 years attending sessional care. The only common additional requirement was for providers to take out insurance, which is advised rather than required in the Guidance.

Certain grey areas in implementing the standards were highlighted by officers, such as what constituted a 'supervised activity', and, more importantly, how to implement aspects of the 'fit person' criteria, especially those relating to whether a person is 'warm' and able to provide care for children of diverse cultural backgrounds. Although authorities had adopted various practices to implement aspects of the 'fit person' criteria, for example, obtaining health checks, police checks or personal references, other aspects were less tangible and more reliant upon discretion. As one officer put it:

> *'It's using your own judgement . . . It's very difficult . . . Are we refusing to register someone because the person is not 'warm' when we may have visited them when no children are present?'*

In general the equal opportunities aspects of the Act, including that relating to assessments of 'fitness', although broadly welcomed, were often perceived to be difficult to put into practice. Officers often reported a lack of understanding of the issues among providers, and sometimes felt that they themselves needed more training or experience in this area. Officers in some authorities also expressed the view that the issue of ethnic diversity was not something that could be imposed like other standards, but involved educating providers to increase awareness. The issue of equal opportunities is discussed further in Chapter 6.

**Re-registration**

A statutory requirement was placed on local authorities to re-register existing provision under the new system within a year of implementation. Our evidence suggested that this was a difficult deadline for local authorities to comply with. Seven of the English authorities and only one Welsh authority completed registration within the statutory timescale. A large number of others had completed the bulk of re-registration by this time but had outstanding provision to re-register. Volume of work and staffing difficulties were given as the reasons for non-completion by the majority of those who did not complete on time.

A number of authorities reported a loss of child-minders as a result of the re-registration exercise, sometimes representing as much as 25% or more of the original list. In most cases this was said to be a consequence of the number of inactive child-minders on existing registers. Although some loss of child-minders remains unexplained, it seems clear that the process of re-registration had been seen by authorities as being as much about bringing registers up-to-date and finding out what provision existed in their areas as about applying the new standards.

Very few cases of refusal or cancellation of registration were reported among the authorities. The majority of authorities described themselves as flexible and allowing time for providers to meet the new standards was seen as a key element in this flexible approach. As one officer summarised:

*'What we were focusing on was the facility's commitment to move towards meeting the standards at some point, rather than feeling that everything had to be in place.'*

**The response of providers**

The general perception of officers interviewed was that the transition to the new system had been a difficult one for some providers. However, this was reported less in authorities which had a well-developed registration system in place before the Act. These difficulties varied from initial anxieties among providers or groups of providers, to outright conflict and hard lobbying against the standards. The points of conflict with providers most commonly mentioned included: the staff:child ratios; the staff qualification requirements; the cost of making physical improvements to premises; and, in the case of the private sector, the commercial viability of running the facility under the new standards. Extremes of conflict were reported in only four authorities; others felt that they had managed to contain and allay the fears of providers by consultation and by adopting the accommodating and flexible approach urged in Circular 1/93.

**Support, training and advice**

The Act gives local authorities the power to provide a range of forms of support to day care providers including *'training, advice and counselling'* (Guidance, para. 4.1). It recognises that such support is an element in enabling the provision of good quality services and facilitating the provision of services within the independent sector. Despite this, almost no authorities had an established policy on training or support for day care workers, although in some authorities the review had highlighted the need for support.

Local authority officers felt that the reorganisation of the regulation function had some implications for the support available to providers. In the 10 authorities which had put registration and inspection tasks in independent units, there was generally a clear split between the regulation role and the support role, which most officers believed would avoid any conflict of interest between the two. Some staff in inspection units, however, did envisage a limited support role as part of their duties. In some of the authorities with independent inspection, staff outside the units felt that the move to independent inspection had diminished the availability of local support and that the reorganisation of staff had left it unclear who had responsibility for proffering support to providers.

In the authorities where regulation was left with under-8s workers, the value of local knowledge and support as part of the regulation process was acknowledged but, in practice, many staff felt that they had little time to offer support as distinct from regulation because of the increase in their workload. Although some of those involved did express the view that the situation might be eased in future years, the more general view to emerge was that the new regulatory system was felt to have reduced the provision of support by increasing the priority given to regulation without replacing the attendant loss of resources for support. By contrast, in a few authorities where there had previously been little or no support, it was felt that the extra attention given to day care by the Children Act had led to an increase in the amount of support available to providers.

The amount of training available varied considerably both between and within authorities. Some authorities offered a wide range of training courses, but others offered very little. Most training for independent providers was provided by (or in conjunction with) the voluntary sector – PPA, Mudiad Ysgolion Meithrin (MYM) and National Child-minding Association (NCMA). Where authorities were decentralised into a number of districts, the different areas were not always consistent in the amount of training that was available. Several authorities provided pre-registration training, particularly for child-minders, and many made this a condition of registration. However, the extent of this training varied enormously, from one half-day session upwards. It was generally agreed that existing child-minders who were being re-registered could not be required to attend. A survey by the NCMA in one local authority found that the majority of child-minders said they had received no training or support from the local authority. Where local forums existed, these would generally emphasise the desire for more training of day care workers – especially child-minders. In a few local authorities, training was targeted at child-minders willing to take children sponsored by the local authority. Seven authorities proposed measures in their review to improve support, mainly training, through resourcing, reviewing or coordinating efforts.

Registration and inspection visits were seen as times when advice could be given, especially if the provision was felt to be below standard. Support was seen as a way of bringing up to standard those providers who did not meet the registration requirements – as an alternative to de-registration. In one case a local authority representative said:

> *'Although [authority] has adopted minimal legal standards, we try to work with providers to agree higher ones and set out how these might be achieved.'*

This was said to be done by advice on good practice.

A few local authorities issued detailed guidance[1] for those seeking registration. This set out not only what was expected for registration, but also what was expected for good practice.

In some authorities small grants were available from an equipment budget: for example, for safety mats, fire blankets, safety film for glass, etc. Some also had equipment for loan. Some made start-up grants to play-groups, and some would subsidise the rent of playgroups' premises. Generally these budgets were under pressure, in some cases having been severely reduced. In some local authorities, day care officers or social workers organised groups for child-minders to meet together. Where this had been done, it was felt to have been useful.

**Quality**

Most local authorities in the study perceived the registration and inspection process to be a key part of their strategy for ensuring quality in services for under 8s. However, none had any accepted definition of quality by which to measure their success. Quality was acknowledged to be difficult to measure or to quantify but related to good practice and involved issues such as adult/child interaction, equal opportunities and parental involvement among others. Local authorities laid different emphases on these quality or good practice issues as part of the regulation process. Some local authorities clearly saw the new system as a way of raising debates about quality and the role of regulation in achieving it.

Six authorities raised proposals in their reviews concerning regulation and quality. Three proposed work to monitor quality, while a fourth referred vaguely to the need to establish *'mechanisms . . . to ensure the ongoing quality of services'*. Two referred to developing joint standards with Education and/or other agencies; one referred to providing money to help services

1.   In at least one case, this document was charged for.

meet requirements; and another to addressing the issue of excessive workload among regulatory staff.

**Assessments of the new system**

Local authorities have, for the most part, welcomed the new regulatory system and devoted a considerable amount of time and resources to its implementation. Among the positive effects reported were: the higher profile it gave to children's services; the greater effectiveness and consistency of the new system and the organisational arrangements; and the raising of standards through the elimination of bad practice as part of the process. Negative comments included those relating to the loss of support and, overwhelmingly, those relating to the apparent undermining of efforts seen to be implicit in Circular 1/93. As the new regulation system got fully under way with the annual inspection of services, a great many authorities felt that they now no longer 'knew where they stood' in relation to enforcing standards.

**Summary**

The Children Act has resulted in substantial reorganisation of the task of regulation in many authorities including the relocation of registration and inspection into independent inspection units. This overhaul of previous arrangements for regulation had often entailed the most significant extra expenditure on children's services arising from the Act. However, the organisational arrangements, staffing arrangements and consequent workloads of inspectors in different authorities were found to vary markedly. Despite some opposition from providers in some authorities, there was little evidence of loss of provision resulting from the new system so far. Most authorities, before receiving Circular 1/93, saw themselves as 'encouraging and flexible'.

# Equal Opportunities and Ethnic Diversity

**Introduction**

In recent years there has been a growing awareness of the importance of positively addressing the needs of all children in Britain's multi-ethnic society. The importance of the early years in a child's development has for some time also been widely recognised. But while it is often assumed that in the early years children are innocent of racial prejudice, research suggests that children as young as three can be aware of simple racial differences and also give different values to them (Milner, 1983; Carrington and Short, 1989).

For children from 'black' and other minority ethnic groups, there is the question of whether services are ethnically sensitive and accessible to them. This assumes greater importance when taken in conjunction with the fact that children from minority ethnic families are disproportionately represented among the UK child population (OPCS, 1992). Additionally, there is an identified greater social need of early years services among them (DHSS, 1984) arising from employment patterns, linguistic differences and so on.

In the Children Act the principle of equal opportunities and issues relating to ethnic diversity have gained a place in children's legislation for the first time. Under its provisions local authorities are given a statutory obligation to *'have regard to the different racial groups to which children within their area who are in need belong'* (Schedule 2, para. 11) when making arrangements for provision of day care services for children in need. Moreover, when deciding whether to cancel registration on the grounds that the care provided is *'seriously inadequate having regards to the [child's] needs'*, local authorities are required to *'have regard to the child's religious persuasion, racial origin, and cultural and linguistic background'* when considering what those needs are (Section 74(1)(b), (2)(b) and (6)). This concern with equal opportunities for ethnic minorities is further emphasised in the Act's supporting Guidance. The general principles which the Guidance proposes should inform good practice in day care include the following:

*'children should be treated and respected as individuals'*

*'the values deriving from different backgrounds – racial, cultural, religious and linguistic – should be recognised and respected'* (Guidance, para. 6.2).

The framework for the development of children's services provided in the Guidance includes: taking account of a child's 'race', religion, culture and language in determining whether s/he is 'in need' and in assessing need; ensuring the involvement of all ethnic groups in reviewing day care and in developing services locally; keeping data on the ethnic composition of the local population; having approved equal opportunities policies and established systems for monitoring and reviewing their implementation. The Guidance also stresses the importance of enabling children 'to develop positive attitudes to differences of race, culture, and language' (Guidance, para. 6.10). Last, but not least, the Guidance specifies that one of the points that a local authority must have regard to in determining whether someone is 'fit' to look after young children is their 'knowledge of and attitude to multi-cultural issues and people of different racial origin' (Guidance, para. 7.32).

This chapter examines the way in which local authorities have interpreted these principles in implementing the sections of the Children Act relating to under-8s services.

**Equal opportunities in practice**

In general terms there had not been a uniform approach to addressing equal opportunities issues within local authorities, but the extent to which such policies and practices had been developed was often, though not always, related to the proportion of minority ethnic communities within the local population.

The Guidance stipulates that authorities should have approved equal opportunities policies (para. 6.11). Most authorities in our sample had corporate equal opportunities employment policies implemented through personnel departments; but corporate policies relating to service delivery were found in only one Welsh and five English authorities. However, in some authorities individual departments such as Social Services or Education had equal opportunities policies covering all operations.

Equal opportunities policies also need supporting structures, practices and procedures if they are to be effectively implemented. Such structures could be found at member level, at officer level within a central policy-making department, and/or units or dedicated posts at departmental level. Sometimes equal opportunities could form part of an officer's role. One or more of these approaches had been adopted by nine of the English and six of the Welsh authorities in our sample. Equal opportunities issues could, however, be addressed without dedicated posts/units if an institutional framework had been developed. In one inner London authority, no identified equal opportunities post or unit existed, but all development plans were required to have a 'quality and equality' section outlining how these issues were to be addressed. On the other hand, the need for a policy framework within which to operate was exemplified in an outer London borough which had no equal opportunities policies. There, cognisance given to the issue depended on individual officers, and initiatives were consequently isolated and piecemeal.

**Children 'in need'**

In implementing the Children Act, local authorities had to develop criteria which would determine whether a child could be considered to be 'in need'. While there is a danger that identifying minority ethnic children as in need is potentially stigmatising, the interpretation in the Guidance of the relevant section of the Act – that a child's needs should include *'physical, emotional and educational needs according to his race, religion, culture and language'* – is more positive, and allows for a recognition of need arising from racial disadvantage.

The needs of minority ethnic children were not referred to specifically by most of the sample authorities developing 'in need' categories. However, four of the English and two of the Welsh authorities did include such a reference. For example, among the English authorities, discussions and adopted definitions of need relating to minority ethnic families ranged from criteria that identified needs associated with discrimination to those taking a stand against racism in society. These included a northern English county with a small minority ethnic population whose definition of 'in need' included children who were *'disadvantaged through deprivation and/or discrimination'*. An Inner London borough with a high minority ethnic population went further, and included *'children whose ethnic, cultural, and/ or religious background exposes them to identified discrimination, harassment and hardship'* among their priority groups for allocation of resources.

However, inclusion of minority ethnic children within 'in need' categories was not entirely unproblematic. For instance, a southern English county with a small minority ethnic population had developed a definition to include those *'whose health or development is likely to be significantly impaired as a result of cultural or racial or religious factors'*. An officer in that authority spoke of the difficulty they had had in arriving at a wording that did not identify all minority ethnic children as in need, but still recognised the possibility of racial disadvantage.

In Wales, the highest minority ethnic population in any local authority area is under 5% of the total, and without officer and/or member support, minority ethnic issues could remain in the background. Among our sample, one authority (with a relatively high minority ethnic population) had appointed a consultant to look into the needs of minority ethnic families; and in a rural authority with a very small minority ethnic population the question of whether children from its 'black' community should be included as being 'in need' because of racial discrimination had been discussed in a multi-agency group. However, such a category did not feature in the authority's final document.

Overall, the needs of minority ethnic children were considered as part of the 'in need' criteria of just a few of the sample authorities, both in England and in Wales. Factors other than the size of the minority ethnic population have influenced the development of policy.

**The review of early years services**

In its role as coordinator, a local authority is expected to conduct a review of day care and related services in its area, as discussed in Chapter 3. Most authorities whose reviews were available had given some consideration to equal opportunities issues, as shown in Table 6.1. In the review reports of one English and two Welsh authorities no mention was made of minority ethnic families or of equal opportunities. Six reviews identified specific issues concerning ethnic minorities: four proposed improved information on use of services (e.g. better monitoring); three proposed measures to encourage greater usage of services; three proposed the development of consultation with ethnic minority groups; and three raised other specific issues.

The involvement of minority ethnic families in the review process was attempted, though in different ways, by eight English and one Welsh authority in our sample. As shown in Table 6.1, a small number of authorities had representation from minority ethnic groups or organisations such as Race Equality Councils on their review steering groups, but the majority attempted to reach minority ethnic families in the review consultation process. Attempts at consultation ranged from a questionnaire to all homes in one council area to consultation with local Race Equality Councils and invited meetings with minority ethnic organisations. Despite many authorities reporting that they had put a great deal of effort into such consultation, it was acknowledged to be largely unsuccessful.

**Table 6.1  Issues Relating to Ethnic Diversity and the review process in the sampled authorities**

| Issues raised | Sample authorities categorised by percentage population of minority ethnic groups | | | | | | | | | | | | | | | | Total |
|---|---|---|---|---|---|---|---|---|---|---|---|---|---|---|---|---|---|
| | 0–5% | | | | 6–10% | | | | 11–15% | | | | over 15% | | | | |
| | EC | EM | L | W | EC | EM | L | W | EC | EM | L | W | EC | EM | L | W | |
| Needs of minority ethnic families mentioned in review document | 7 | 3 | | 3 | | 2 | | | | | | | | 1 | 2 | | 18 |
| Data on ethnic composition/dispersion provided | 4* | 2* | | 3 | | 2 | | | | | | | | 1 | 2 | | 14 |
| Ethnic monitoring of providers and/or service take-up undertaken/planned | 1 | | | 1 | | | | | | | | | | 1 | 2 | | 5 |
| Minority ethnic representations on review steering group | 1 | 1 | | | | | | | | | | | | | | | 2 |
| REC reps on review steering group | 1 | | | | | | | | | | | | | | 1 | | 2 |
| Other consultation with minority ethnic families in review process | 4 | 1 | | 1 | | | | | | | | | | 1 | 1 | | 8 |
| No consultation with or mention of minority ethnic communities in review | | | | 2 | | | 1 | | | | | | | | | | 3 |

KEY: EC = English county councils; EM = English metropolitan authorities; L = London authorities; W = Welsh authorities

\* includes one authority which identified need for such data

Difficulties with consultation did not appear to be related to the consultation strategy used, but to a deeper issue, as the experience of a metropolitan authority suggests. There, when consultation with its large minority ethnic population was being planned, the advice of the officer dealing with matters of 'race' and equal opportunities in the implementing department was that the authority's minority ethnic population felt 'suspicious and hostile' towards the council and that an adequate mechanism for consulting with the 'black' community needed to be developed after careful consideration of the issue. This view has been endorsed in Elfer and McQuail's evaluation project on local authority reviews (Elfer and McQuail, forthcoming), and is supported in the literature on consultation (Christie and Blunden, 1991; Gaister and Martin, 1993; Gill, 1985; Qaiyoom, 1992).

Other important issues relating to ethnic diversity were also highlighted in the reviews. Data from a limited monitoring of the use of services by minority ethnic families in some of the reviews identified a low take-up of services, and a disproportionately low level of minority ethnic providers in some authorities. In authorities with very small minority ethnic populations, the particular problems relating to a mainly white area were identified. This issue had been considered in the review of one northern authority, in which the dimensions of the problem are discussed, and included the following:

- a lack of minority ethnic group representation on groups involved in making early years policy

- a lack of training and experience in dealing with racism in children's services

- a lack of services specifically addressing the needs of individual minority ethnic groups

- a lack of realistic experiences of ethnic diversity for white children.

**Regulation and support**

In registration requirements prior to the Children Act, equal opportunities issues figured only through the operation of the 1976 Race Relations Act. The implications of the Act and Guidance for regulation and equal opportunities were therefore new in many areas for both local authorities and providers.

Attempting to put into practice such principles as the fit person criteria relating to equal opportunities, however, presented practical problems. The most common approach found among the sample authorities (eleven

English and three Welsh) was to place a requirement on providers to sign an equal opportunities statement or declaration prior to registration, or to have an equal opportunities policy, in an effort to ensure non-discriminatory services. Other approaches to the issue included discussing its implications in inspection visits or as part of an authority's support function, and placing a pre-registration training requirement (which included equal opportunities training) on prospective child-minders. A result of enforcing these criteria in one authority was that a few child-minders were not re-registered because of their attitudes to non-discriminatory care.

In general equal opportunities was considered to be one of the more intangible, qualitative issues within regulation and often noted as some-thing to be addressed more fully when the re-registration deadline had been met. Authorities with a very low minority ethnic population reported a lack of understanding among providers about the relevance of equal opportunities to their service. In more than one such authority officers also made comments that point to how little they themselves understood the issue – a finding also replicated in Cowley's research on registration and inspection of day care (Cowley, 1993). Indeed, as noted in Chapter 5, inspection staff acknowledged a lack of training and experience in this field, and many saw a particular role for the local authority in providing training both for registration staff and for providers.

**Summary**

The attention given to aspects of equal opportunities in the Children Act has prompted important developments in some local authorities. How-ever, the needs of minority ethnic children have been considered in the 'in need' criteria of only a few of the sample authorities. The review exercise pinpointed major difficulties in consulting with minority ethnic communi-ties which need to be addressed with sensitivity. The low take-up of services by minority ethnic children highlighted in some reviews suggests the need for ethnic monitoring to ascertain whether services are reaching all sectors of the population. Additionally, problems specific to largely 'white' areas which have been identified also need to be addressed.

Our research suggests that while much remains to be done, the Act has had a positive impact in the area of equal opportunities in terms of highlighting issues and raising awareness – in some cases making authorities consider equal opportunities issues in early years services for the first time. How this might affect actual practices or the provision of services is not yet clear.

# The Children Act in Rural Areas

**Introduction**

The Children Act recognises individual diversity - for instance, in children's ethnic and cultural backgrounds – but makes little mention of geographical diversity and the issues that are raised by implementing the Children Act in rural areas. This has been a particular focus of the study in Wales. This chapter considers the themes we have identified in the Children Act, as it relates to children under 8, from a rural perspective.

The discretion given by the Act to local authorities to interpret their requirements in the light of their local situation provides the opportunity to address the particular needs of rural children. Local authorities are expected: to define their own criteria for allocating services to children in need and to decide on an 'appropriate' range of services to meet local needs; to set their own standards for registration of day care services based on government guidelines; and to provide support and training as they see fit (Section 18).

This chapter looks at how far that opportunity had been taken a year after the Children Act came into force. It is based on information gathered in the 13 local authorities in the studies (seven in England, six in Wales) which were designated as rural on the basis of including at least one district with below average population density for England and Wales (3.2 persons per hectare - 1991 Census data). More detail on the definition of 'rural areas' is given elsewhere (Statham and Cameron, 1994).

**Awareness of the needs of rural areas**

Rural Strategies could play a key role in raising awareness of the particular needs of children in rural areas. However, in only one of the 13 authorities was a senior children's services manager aware of a county-wide Rural Strategy document which made reference to the needs of rural families. Such documents have tended to focus on topics related to conservation and land use, and frequently fail to address social and economic issues (Clark, 1992).

Awareness had been raised, however, by the new duty given to local authorities by the Children Act to review the services which are available to children under 8, and to publish a report on this as the basis for local planning of children's services. Analysis of the first reviews produced by the local authorities in the study suggests that these documents are indeed serving to highlight uneven levels of provision, including the lack of services for children in rural areas. Most authorities provided a break-down of type of service by district (either council districts or Social Services areas), although in some cases where these districts covered both rural areas and a large town, the analysis was not detailed enough to indicate significant differences between them. Half of the authorities containing rural districts referred specifically to the lower level of service there, especially in the provision of nursery classes and full day care, although few went beyond stating this fact to suggesting how it could be rectified.

The short timescale for completion of the first review meant that consul-tation had often been limited at this stage. As discussed in Chapter 3 the review duty appeared to be stimulating the setting up or revitalising of early years liaison groups or forums, especially in Wales where few existed before the Act. Progress was still at an early stage; local early years forums were often established in only some districts in a county, and these did not always have a clear channel to make their voice heard. However, most authorities in the study had plans to encourage the development of such groups as a result of the review. Provided local forums have a clear structure for influencing policy-makers and planners (for instance, through feeding information to a county-level forum which sends a representative to a county planning or strategy group), they should be well placed to highlight the particular circumstances of their local area and thus to ensure that rural needs are not overlooked.

**Are rural children 'in need'?**

Although the needs of all children living in rural areas may have been made more visible, this does not guarantee that they will be met. The duty placed on local authorities to provide services for children in need means that the way in which need is defined is crucial in determining whether a child has access to services (as discussed in Chapter 4). The popular conception of an idyllic rural childhood suggests such children are not in need. This is beginning to be challenged by research which has demon-strated the difficulties rural families may face, including isolation, material deprivation, lack of support and few opportunities for children to socialise with their peers (Archbishops' Commission on Rural Areas, 1990; Essle-mont and Harrington, 1991; Palmer, 1991).

However, only one of the thirteen authorities in the study included *'children whose development is significantly impaired by rural isolation'* as a specific indicator of need. Other criteria which authorities had adopted often had an urban bias, such as overcrowding, proportion of single parents, high levels of unemployment and numbers of children receiving free school meals. These may work against the development of services in rural areas. Five of the local authorities in the study made specific reference in the review or in other policy documents to the possible negative consequences for rural areas of using particular socio-economic deprivation indicators to define 'in need neighbourhoods' or to site new nursery classes. At the time the interviews were carried out it was too early to say whether these fears were likely to be realised; most authorities had defined their criteria for need, but as Chapter 4 points out, this had not yet resulted in any significant changes in the group who received services.

**Appropriate models of rural early years services**

The typically lower levels of provision in rural areas, especially publicly funded services such as council day nurseries and nursery education (Owen and Moss, 1989; Rural Development Commission, 1992; Stone, 1990), create problems both for local authorities in meeting their duty to provide for children in need, and for parents in finding accessible services. Models of local authority provision suitable for urban areas, such as a family centre serving a large estate or a day nursery based in the town, are likely to be inappropriate in a sparsely populated area, and there is a need to develop innovative ways of delivering services. The rural authorities in the study were asked how they had tried to meet the needs of children living in isolated areas, and whether they had any plans to develop new kinds of provision to reach such children. The overall impression was of piecemeal development, often dependent on the energies of particular individuals rather than any coherent planning of services for children in rural areas. Officers commonly perceived levels of provision in rural areas as inadequate, and a number of authorities had plans for how services to young children could be developed. These included:

- community child-minding schemes, where the authority recruits, trains and pays minders to take nominated children

- additional sponsored places in community play groups and private day nurseries

- outreach work from existing family centres or local authority playgroups

- employment of Under-8s Development Workers in each district to help set up and support local community initiatives such as parent and toddler groups and holiday play schemes

- development of mobile provision such as playbuses, in partnership with local voluntary organisations

- grants to voluntary organisations to cover the cost of providing transport for isolated children to attend services

- clustering of small schools for nursery provision

- providing a low-cost resource base to coordinate and support existing local initiatives; for instance, by converting a council house.

A common feature of most of these models of service delivery is the support and development of local, community-based, open-access provision, rather than offering specialist services restricted to children in need. It also relies on partnerships between agencies, especially the voluntary and statutory sectors. However, many of the above plans had not been approved for funding at the time of the fieldwork, and officers commonly expressed fears that, in the context of limited resources and a duty to provide for children in need, such developments were unlikely to be accorded a high priority.

**Inspecting and supporting rural day care services**

Services in rural areas are likely to face a particular challenge in meeting the new standards for registration and inspection by Social Services (see Chapter 5). Playgroups are a particularly important form of provision for children in the countryside, but most are under-resourced and meet in premises that are not designed specifically for young children, such as village halls (Brophy, Statham and Moss, 1992). Yet the consequences of closing down playgroups in rural areas would be particularly severe, in many cases leaving children with no alternative provision at all.

As Chapter 5 notes, the initial re-registration period has not resulted in the closure of services, although this needs to be reassessed in the light of the first annual inspection, as providers were often given time to bring themselves up to the new standards. Some registration officers in rural areas reported taking into account the particular circumstances of rural services – for instance, by allowing bowls instead of fixed handbasins and properly sited portable toilets instead of plumbed-in facilities in the case of rural playgroups meeting in a poorly serviced village hall. Such flexibility avoided the loss of a much-needed local service, but there is clearly a danger of creating a two-tier service where lower standards are tolerated in rural provision because any service is seen as better than none. An awareness of the particular circumstances of rural providers needs to go hand-in-hand with better support for rural groups to enable them to reach standards and develop good quality provision. This could mean help with meeting physical standards (e.g. grants to fund necessary improvements, help with finding alternative premises) or advice and support for workers (e.g. peripatetic support staff, better training opportunities which include cover so that workers are able to attend courses).

There were some example among local authorities of attempts to provide such support to rural services, but these were not widespread. Officers commonly reported particular difficulties in organising training and support for day care providers in rural areas of the county, including the long distances for providers to travel on poor roads and the need to cancel courses because of bad weather. Branches of support organisations and training courses were generally located in towns. As discussed in Chapter 5, the ability of Social Services staff to support and develop day care services had frequently been undermined by reorganisation or the additional workload of registration and inspection. In these circumstances, the dilemma of raising standards in independent services without forcing them to close is likely to remain a particularly acute one in rural areas.

**Summary**

The impact of the Children Act on services for children in rural areas appeared to be pulling in two opposite directions. On the one hand, it has served to raise the profile of the needs of rural families. The review exercise has highlighted gaps and inequalities in levels of provision, and the setting up of local under-8s networks has created a potential for taking these issues forward and keeping rural issues on the agenda. The emphasis in the Guidance on local, accessible provision, on non-stigmatising services and on agencies working together, all reinforce ways of working which are good models generally but are particularly appropriate in rural areas. Rural authorities are particularly well placed to take the lead in showing how services which have been artificially separated can be brought together and in putting the coordination aspects of the Act into practice.

On the other hand, the duty to provide services for children in need, in the context of limited resources, creates the danger that although the needs of rural children have been made more visible, nothing will be done about their situation because of the principle of targeting resources on those who are most in need. Only one authority specified rural isolation as a criterion of 'in need', and other criteria often had an urban bias which may work against the development of services in rural areas. The research also indicated a particular need to develop ways of providing training and support to early years workers in rural areas.

Chapter

# 8    Conclusions and Discussion

**Introduction**

The first year of implementing the Act presented local authorities with new challenges and opportunities for under-8s services. The ways in which local authorities have responded to these is as variable as the points from which they started in terms of the history of early years provision and policy. However, the general picture to emerge at this stage is one of some significant achievements, although certain outcomes of implementation are still uncertain and remain issues to be taken forward by local authorities. These will be looked at in the second stage of the research. Finally, there are also constraints to be addressed if the Children Act is to achieve its full potential and if early years services are to develop and flourish. These achievements, issues for the future and constraints are discussed in turn in this closing chapter.

**Achievements**

In general, the Act was widely welcomed by local authority staff involved in under-8s services. The general perception was that the Act had put services for young children 'on the map' and had gone some way to ending their historically marginal role. It was also widely seen as an opportunity for local authorities to review a range of policies, provision and procedures relating to under-8s services: as one officer in a Social Services Department concluded, *'the Children Act has made us take a good look at what we're doing'.*

More specifically, the Act has given local authority staff the opportunity to review the way in which services they provide are appropriate for children in need in their area and at how access to such services might be prioritised. Local authorities have also been encouraged, both through the duty to identify the extent of need and in the completion of the first review, to take an overview of how local provision matches local needs. As one officer put it:

> *'The Children Act has not led to a growth in provision but a raising of awareness, including the need to look at what we've got and how we can use it.'*

These opportunities have contributed to a recognition of the need for information systems to contribute to the planning of future early years services. The new triennial review duty was recognised in most authorities as being a welcome innovation of the Act and the cornerstone of the strategy for providing the information required to plan early years services. In practice, producing the review was often thought to have been a more limited exercise than originally envisaged. But some authorities, including the following one which had created a dedicated post to complete the review, believed the process to have been highly successful:

> 'The review has highlighted the importance of day care. People at a senior level have had a change of mind.'

It was clear that the emphasis placed on coordination in all aspects of service planning and delivery within the Act and Guidance had acted as a stimulant to greater interdepartmental communication, either through the use of existing coordinating structures, or collaboration in drawing up the review. The stimulus provided by the Act to joint working was one of the most widely noted benefits of the first year:

> 'Before the Act, we hardly knew these people . . . Leisure and Amenities were something in the distance; now they are very much part of our working day. People don't think Social Services any more, they think of this group of people.'

> 'We're working together; bridges are being built; joint initiatives are being discussed and put into action.'

> 'The Act has built bridges between agencies that weren't there before, created networks of people, strengthened the voluntary sector . . .'

It was in the area of regulation that perhaps the greatest changes in practice have been achieved as a result of the Act. Many authorities had substantially reorganised and reviewed the resourcing of this aspect of under-8s services, and felt that their systems and procedures were improved as a result; this was the area where most extra resources made available for implementation had been placed. An overall feeling that improved regulatory processes could help to improve the quality of services was found among local authority staff involved in regulation.

> 'In the old system under-8s day care provision came bottom of Social Services' list . . . now it has a much higher profile. The work of under-5s advisers was very much under-valued before. The new arrangements will raise the status of day care providers.'

> 'It's enhanced expectations of provision . . . Quality has become a real issue now. The new regulations have really focused providers.'

The Act's recognition of diversity among different groups of children has stimulated renewed interest in how all aspects of equal opportunities policies relate to work with young children, and some authorities have, in response to the Act, considered the needs of children from different ethnic groups, some for the first time. The need to recognise diversity among both children and parents was found to cut across all three functions of local authorities in terms of under 8s, and examples were found of authorities exploring new ways of making services more responsive to minority ethnic groups, consulting with them about the planning and delivery of services, and incorporating aspects of equal opportunities policies into policies on provision for children in need and policies on regulation.

Finally, several aspects of the Act, including the need to review and to coordinate services, have offered the potential for local authorities to take account of the particular needs of children from rural areas and to develop models of service delivery appropriate to their needs.

The enthusiasm with which the Act was greeted resulted in a great deal of time and energy being invested in efforts to turn the promise of the legislation into effective policies and practice; many of the successful aspects of implementation depended on this investment, rather than new resources being made available. Ultimately, however, the impact of the Act was highly dependent on where local authorities started from in terms of the way in which they organised under-8s services, the levels of provision in different sectors and the historical and political commitment to under-8s services. In authorities which described themselves as starting from a low base in terms of commitment to early years services, the Act was often thought to have had a significantly beneficial impact, as the following respondent described:

> 'Given our starting position, the authority has done remarkably well. We had a poor resource base, [an] inward looking culture, and have now attracted more resources, a tighter management structure, begun to look outwards and to develop joint planning.'

In other authorities, the Act was seen either as less significant compared to existing policies (this was very apparent, for example, in the authority where all services had been integrated within the Education Department) or as confirming and perhaps reinforcing existing policy and practice:

> 'The Act gave a head of steam to issues already on the agenda.'

> 'The Children Act was great backing for things we'd been saying for years.'

The achievements of the Act in its initial phase were therefore far from uniform among our sample. The diversity of approaches among local authorities to implementing the Act and the results achieved in different aspects of implementation were as diverse as the history and approaches to under-8s services which predated the Act. Nor do we have the full picture of outcomes and achievements of implementation at this early stage. Many of the processes involved in implementing the Act involve long-term policy objectives, the achievement of which is a matter for ongoing evaluation. A general feeling was expressed by local authority officers that the long-term impact of implementation had yet to be felt and that the first year had enabled agendas to be set up and identification of issues to be tackled in the future as the following respondent expressed:

> 'The authority is getting there. Plans have taken a long time to reach fruition . . . There are things to build on.'

**Outstanding issues and future research questions**

After the first year of the Act's implementation, local authorities were still at an early stage in reviewing policies and procedures and meeting the multiple demands of the new legislation. In carrying out the first review, for example, many local authorities had felt forced to complete a hasty and less than comprehensive exercise in order to meet the statutory timetable for completion. In such authorities there was often a recognition of the need for a more thorough process when completing the second review. The review itself implies an ongoing process and recommendations leading to tangible results in the longer term. How local authorities carry forward their next review duty in the light of lessons learnt from the first is therefore an issue for further exploration.

One purpose of the Section 19 review is to support a more coordinated approach to services, involving both local authority departments and other organisations. The implementation of the Act and the review itself had led both to more working together and proposals for new structures to support coordination in the future. It will be important to see how far this interest converts into new structures and to what extent coordination moves from talking together to acting together, through joint planning, joint policies or joint services, or the pooling of resources to support a coordinated approach. Also, it is apparent that a coordinated approach requires resourcing, both in terms of people to enable the process and of funding to support them and the whole process of working together. It remains to be seen whether rhetoric and commitment will be backed by the necessary means.

Although it was clear that substantial organisational changes had occurred in the way that local authorities were carrying out their regulatory role in response to the Act, the impact of such changes on the actual practice of regulation is not yet clear. The new functions of the local authority with respect to inspection as well as registration were barely embarked upon at the time of first stage visits to authorities. At this stage a general feeling of uncertainty existed among local authority staff about the status of the advice given in the Guidance and their role in enforcing good practice as a result of both the Circular 1/93 and the then pending high court decision on the case of the Sutton child-minder who had challenged the way in which the local authority had applied its 'no smacking policy' to her registration. The high court has subsequently upheld the appeal of the child-minder. The impact of the new system, and the different ways in which it is organised and resourced in different local authorities is therefore something which requires considerable further investigation and should of course include the views of those being regulated as well as the regulators themselves.

The Guidance envisages regulation playing a major role in improving quality. Whether and how regulation is applied to this end, and whether it is possible to assess the impact are major issues. An important factor here will be the extent to which local authorities provide support to complement regulation, and how the regulatory duty and support powers relate in practice. Of particular importance will be the impact on this relationship of the different ways in which local authorities have organised regulation: for example, if it has been placed in an independent inspection unit.

The provision duty under the Act is closely involved with how local authorities interpret 'in need' and how they then proceed to identify and assess children who meet the criteria. Will day care services be used on an increasing scale for children 'in need', and will there be a sufficient supply of adequately prepared services? How will local authorities ensure such a supply? And to what extent will local authorities use their power to provide services for children not 'in need'? The different starting points of local authorities will be particularly important here, not only because of existing differences in supply, but also because it will be important to observe what happens in authorities which adopt a broad definition of 'in need' or else have aspired to develop universal services for all children. While, in the private sector, we need to know whether the Act will promote expansion of supply (for example, via the review process) or constrain expansion (for example, through the regulatory function).

The area of equal opportunities or ethnic/cultural/linguistic diversity, as previously noted, was an innovatory aspect of the Act. As such, it was one which involved many local authorities in addressing for the first time issues such as how they might consult with different minority ethnic communities on under-8s issues, how services provided should reflect the needs of different ethnic groups and how equal opportunities issues could be implemented more generally as part of the regulation process. Although some local authorities had well developed existing policies in this area, it was new ground for many others. At this stage, while there is evidence of a general raising of awareness among local authorities about equal opportunities issues and an acknowledgement of the difficulties involved in consultation, how this might eventually translate into policy or impact on practice is not yet clear and will remain an issue in the evaluative stage of the project.

This report leaves local authorities at a point where there are many outstanding issues, many of which we hope to address in the second stage of our research. However, it is important to emphasise that it will not be easy to make a clear assessment of the Act's impact on services for young children. First, because on many issues no clear data exist on the situation before implementation. To take an obvious example, without agreed definitions of quality applied before implementation and then again afterwards, the consequences of the Act for quality will remain uncertain. Second, because the Act does not occur in a vacuum, it is not always clear what to attribute to the Act and what to other influences. Ultimately, the Act is just one of many factors which determine which services of what quality are available to which children.

**Constraints**

In Chapter 1, we outlined part of the context within which the Act was implemented. This context is important for many reasons. It is essential for assessing the significance, limitations and opportunities of the Act and therefore for interpreting the results of research on the Act. It also helps to identify factors that may support or constrain taking advantage of the opportunities and aspirations contained in the Act and Guidance. Neither a descriptive account of the implementation of the Act, such as this report, nor a more evaluative exercise, such as that we are now embarked upon, can avoid recognising several contextual factors which may constrain full realisation of the objectives contained in the Act and Guidance. We conclude with three examples.

First, the concern with promoting coordination is not assisted by other legislative and government developments. Reforms in the Health and Education services make it harder to coordinate with these key agencies. For example, recent Education reforms have the effect of:

*'working against soundly-based planning and cooperation among agencies . . . We see in the [Education] legislation an ambivalence about strategic planning, a demand-led approach to resource management, a preference to respond to the views of parents but not children and a strong commitment to market forces' (Cracknell, 1992).*

Equally problematic is the growing involvement in day care services of TECS, Economic Development Units, the Department of Employment and other agencies primarily concerned with employment and business which has produced a third force with a major interest in 'early childhood services' – in addition to Social Services and Education. The problem is not that there are more parties involved. The problem is that each party has its own agenda; each party is concerned with one particular group of children or one particular function of service, each party has its own concept of what services are about (support for families 'in need', 'nursery education' for 3- and 4-year-olds, 'child care for working parents'). Above all, these particular agendas, concerns and concepts operate without any unifying policy, centre of responsibility, shared direction or holistic view of the child. Significantly, there is no national review of services involving the key parties to match the local reviews required of local authorities. The recent interest of the Department of Social Security in subsidising the 'day care' costs of low-income, employed parents, and the Prime Minister's office in 'nursery education' promises yet further proliferation and fragmentation of activity.

Attempts at coordination at a local level must be set in the context of the absence of any coherent and coordinated policy and implementation strategy at national level. One officer in a Social Services Department described the effect of this at local level thus:

*'The Children Act is a good piece of legislation, but what the local authority can do, while there is so little political will at the centre and such low status for children's services, is minimal.'*

Second, the ability of regulation to improve quality is likely to be constrained when day care services depend on parental ability to pay and when that ability to pay varies markedly because of large differences in family income as well as other circumstances (for example, number of children in a family). If regulation is applied stringently to improve quality, costs will need to increase; there is a risk then that some services will close because parents cannot pay the additional costs involved or that access will be limited to higher income families. But if regulation is not strongly applied to improve quality, then large differences in quality will emerge, with poorer quality services being used mainly by lower income families. There appears to be a major tension or fault line in the Act and Guidance between provision policy for children not in need, (which is based on unsubsidised private markets and the idea that day care services are market commodities consumed by parents who can and should make trade-offs between quality and cost) and a regulatory policy, most clearly expressed in the Guidance (which is more child-oriented and concerned with the child's needs irrespective of parents' financial resources).

At present, relatively low costs are achieved by many playgroups and child-minders and some private nurseries through poor pay and employment conditions for workers, low levels of training and inferior physical environments. While the Children Act advocates a general promotion of quality as part of the local authorities' role, and encourages them to provide a range of support, training and advice for providers, it does not address the question of how local authorities might resource the improvements of the existing poorly resourced infrastructure of early childhood services, which will continue to impede the promotion of quality in services. Lack of resources – to fund the expansion of provision envisaged in the Act, to offer support to providers to meet standards and to fund improvements required by the new standards – were widely held to be a barrier to more successful implementation of the Act.

> 'The Act itself is a splendid piece of legislation. Its goals are something you'd want to have, but you can't have them without the resources to do it.'

More specifically, there were internal resource issues surrounding local authorities' ability to implement the new duties and powers assigned to them under the Act. These involved staffing levels, existing staff time and training. Evidence at this point suggests that in an overall climate of constraint on such resources, local authorities were finding it difficult to fulfil adequately their duties to regulate services, to coordinate with other busy staff or to undertake the workload involved in the review and the general development of new areas of policy. The effectiveness of implementation will continue to depend not only on the goodwill and enthusiasm of officers, but also on the availability of dedicated staff time to devote to the task.

**The second stage of the Study**

At the end of the first stage of the project we have developed a comprehensive overview of the different local authority approaches to implementing the Children Act for under 8s in England and Wales. We have been impressed by the sheer diversity of approach. Certain common themes have emerged through this picture of variation. These themes now need to be explored in the evaluative stage of the study. Most importantly, this stage will extend to providers themselves, as well as a range of other interested organisations in the voluntary and business sectors. This will afford a unique opportunity to capture the workings of one aspect of this *'comprehensive and far-reaching reform of child care law.'*

# References

Archbishops' Commission on Rural Areas (1990), *Faith in the Countryside*, London: Churchman Publishing

Bradshaw, J. (1990), *Child Poverty and Deprivation in the UK*, (Innocent: Occasional Papers, No. 8), Florence: UNICEF

Bridgwood, A. and Savage, D. (1993), *General Household Survey 1993*, London: HMSO

Brophy, J., Statham, J. and Moss, P. (1992), *Playgroups in Practice: Self-help and Public Policy*, London: HMSO

Carrington, B. and Short, G. (1989), *'Race' and the Primary School: Theory into Practice*, Windsor: NFER-Nelson

Christie, Y. and Blunden, R. (1991), *Is Race on your Agenda*? London: King's Fund

Clark, D. (1992), *'Rural Development Strategies in England'*, paper presented to the conference of the Royal Town Planning Institute, November 1992

Cornia, G. (1993), *Child Poverty and Deprivation in Industrialised Countries: Recent Trends and Policy Options*, (Innocent: Occasional Papers, No. 2), Florence: UNICEF

Cowley, L. (1993), *Registration and Inspection of Daycare for Young Children*, London: NCB

Cracknell, D. (1992), 'Learning in the Market: Recap on Current Educational Developments', in Sassoon, D. (ed.), *Getting our Acts Together: A Report of a Conference Held in London on 22/10/92*, London: National Children's Bureau and Society of Education Officers

Department of Education and Science (1992), *Pupils under Five Years in each Local Authority in England – January 1991 (Statistical Bulletin 5/92)*, London: Department of Education and Science

Department for Education (1993), *Pupils under Five Years of Age in Schools in England – January 1992 (Statistical Bulletin 11/93)*, London: Department for Education

Department of Health (1991), *Guidance and Regulations (Vol. 2): Family Support, Daycare and Educational Provision for Young Children*, London: HMSO

Department of Health (1993a), *Children Act Report 1992* (Cm 2144), London: HMSO

Department of Health (1993b), *Children's Day Care Facilities at 31 March 1992: England*, London: Department of Health

Department of Health and Social Security (1984), *Services for Under Fives from Ethnic Minority Communities*. London: DHSS

Education Select Committee (House of Commons) (1985), *Educational Provision for the Under Fives (Vol. 2)* London: HMSO

Elfer, P. (1993), 'Standing by Standards', *Co-ordinate, May*, 35

Elfer, P. and Beasley, G. (1991), *Registration of Childminding and Day Care: Using the Law to Improve Standards*. London: HMSO

Elfer, P. and McQuail, S. (forthcoming), *Discussion Paper: Participation of and Consulting with Black and Minority Ethnic Groups as part of the Review Process*, London: NCB

Esslemont, E. and Harrington, J. (1991), *Swings and Roundabouts: The Highs and Lows of Life for Pre-School Children and their Families in Rural Powys*. London: Save the Children Fund

Fox-Harding, L. (1991), 'The Children Act 1989 in Context: Four Perspectives in Child Care Law and Policy Parts I (and II)', *Journal of Social Welfare and Family Law*, 3, pp. 179–93 (and 4, pp. 285–304)

Gaister, L. and Martin, L. (1993), 'Community Care Planning: Collaboration, Co-operation and Equal Opportunities', *Social Services Research*, 2, pp. 1–4

Gill, B.A.G. (1985), *Towards Genuine Consultation: Principles of Community Participation* (Report of Joint CRE/ALAOME Conference on Multicultural Anti-racist Education). London: CRE

Harrop, A. and Moss, P. (1994), 'Working parents: Trends in the 1980s, *Employment Gazette, 102(10)*, pp. 343–352

Kumar, V. (1993), *Poverty and Inequality in the UK: The Effects on Children*. London: National Children's Bureau

Marsh, A. and McKay, S. (1993), 'Families, Work and the Use of Childcare', *Employment Gazette*, August, pp. 361–70

Meltzer, H. (1994), *Day Care Services for Children*, London: HMSO

Milner, D. (1983), *Children and Race – Ten Years On*, London: Ward Lock Education

O'Higgins, M. and Jenkins, S. (1989), '*Poverty in Europe: Estimates for 1975, 1980 and 1988*' paper presented at the seminar on Poverty Statistics in the European Community, October 1989, Nordwijk, the Netherlands

OPCS (1988, *General Household Survey 1986, No. 16*, London: HMSO

OPCS (1992), *1991 Census*, London: Government Statistical Service

OPCS (1993), *General Household Survey 1991, No. 21*, London: HMSO

Owen, C. and Moss, P. (1989), 'Patterns of Pre-school Provision in English Local Authorities', *Journal of Educational Policy*, 4, pp. 309–28

Palmer, J. (1991), *Childcare in Rural Communities*, Edinburgh: HMSO

Pre-school Playgroups Association (1993), *Facts and Figures 1993*, London: PPA

Qaiyoom, R. (1992), *From Crisis to Consensus: A Strategic Approach for Local Government and the Black Voluntary Sector*, London: SIA

Rural Development Commission (1992), *1991 Survey of Rural Services*, London: Rural Development Commission

Statham, J. (1993), *The Children Act and Under 8s in Wales*, London: TCRU

Statham, J. and Cameron, C. (1994), 'Young Children in Rural Areas: Implementing the Children Act', *Children and Society*, 8, 1

Statham, J., Lloyd, E., Moss, R., Melhuish, E., Owen, C. (1990), *Playgroups in a Changing World*, London: HMSO

Stone, M. (1990), *Rural Childcare*, London: Rural Development Commission

*The Children Act 1989*, London: HMSO

Trinder, L. (1993), *Reviewing the Reviews: Day Care for Young Children in Yorkshire and Humberside*, London: Save the Children Fund

Welsh Office (1983), *Activities of Social Services Departments: Year Ending 31/3/82*, Cardiff: Welsh Office

Welsh Office (1988), *Statistics of Education in Wales: Schools, No. 1 1987*, Cardiff: Welsh Office

Welsh Office (1993a), *Activities of Social Services Departments: Year Ending 31/3/92*, Cardiff: Welsh Office

Welsh Office (1993b), *Statistics of Education and Training in Wales: Schools, No. 1*, Cardiff: Welsh Office

Witherspoon, S. and Prior, G. (1991), 'Working Mothers: Free to Choose?', in Jowell, R. (ed.), *British Social Attitudes: The 8th Report*, London: Dartmouth

# Appendix A

## Summary of Interviews in the First Stage of the Study – 1992–93

| Authority type | Social Services Policy | Department Regulation officers | Chief executives | Education department | Leisure department | Elected members | Health authority | Voluntary sector |
|---|---|---|---|---|---|---|---|---|
| | | | | Types of interviewee | | | | |
| County council (7) | 17 | 12 | – | 9 | 2 | 4 | – | 1 |
| Metropolitan borough (6) | 16 | 7 | 2 | 11 | 4 | 2 | – | 1 |
| Inner/Outer London boroughs (5) | 13 | 6 | – | 8 | 3 | – | 1 | – |
| Welsh Counties (8) | 33 | 13 | 2 | 11 | 1 | 2 | – | 1 |

# Interview Guide

1 **Organisational structure**

Social Services Department/Education/other relevant departments
Under-8s services – how are they managed
– decentralisation

2 **Implementation process**

Chronology?
Personnel?
Structure?
Other inputs (e.g. consultants/seminars/literature)

3 **Review**

Chronology/projected completion
Structure/personnel involved
Terms of reference
Consultation
Conclusions
Follow-up arrangements

4 **Coordinated planning and provision**

Impact of Children Act
Effect of other reforms in health education/community care
Special difficulties, e.g. rural areas
Any new/particular structures to manage coordination
Commercial partnership/voluntary sector

5 **Policies on provision of day care and nursery education**

General policy in this area?
Changed priorities for eligibility
Method of service delivery

6 **Children in need**

How are children identified and prioritised?
How are services provided?
Education/special needs
Child protection register

Interdepartmental agreement
Discretionary powers – children not in need

7  **Services currently provided**
Numbers of places available – in need
Not in need
Unmet need?

8  **Information services**
Supply/demand/use of services
Ethnic diversity
Disability
Rural/urban areas
How are services publicised?
Consumer evaluation
Structure, e.g. community/early years forums, resources and referral system
Diversity/multilingual publishing

9  **Regulation (registration and inspection)**
Mandatory/discretionary requirements
'Fitness'/de-registration
Interdepartmental participation
Progress
What is the registration/inspection process?
Changes in responsibility/management
Appropriate workload
Impact of Children Act 1989, e.g. charging for registration
Administrative support
Re-registration/fall-out/rejection rate
What are the problem areas?
Resources
Coordination/conflict with private and voluntary sectors
Are you monitoring how the regulation system is working?

10  **Quality**
How has the local authority defined 'quality'?
On what basis?
What would a really good service look like?
Budget constraints
Other obstacles

## 11 Training and support

The Act gives local authorities the power to provide training and support to its own and independent workers.

How has the Act affected the authority's policy on training and support?

Own workers

Child-minders/playgroup leaders/private nurseries

Nannies/relatives

How is training and support provided?

In-house/contracted in

Resources

Projected forward – how will it continue

## 12 Equal opportunities

The Guidance says (para. 6.11): *'Local authorities should have approved equal opportunities policies including arrangements for monitoring and reviewing progress towards implementation.'*

How has the local authority set about meeting this part of the Guidance on the Act?

What are the local authority's arrangements for monitoring and evaluating its equal opportunities policies in respect of under 8s?

## 13 Rural areas

Providing services in rural areas may pose particular problems.

What have these been?

How are they managed?

Does the local authority have a rural areas strategy/programme?

## 14 Resources

Financial resources

   – children in need

   – children not in need

Estimated requirements to implement policies

## 15 Assessment

What have been the major problems/opportunities?

Looking forward to the next years for under 8s services . . .

Printed in the United Kingdom for HMSO
Dd299980 1/95 C7 G559 10170